Da Fishi Code

All my Best
+
Happy reading!

Dan Brown

DA FISHI CODE

Serious and
Not-So-Serious
Stories from da Rivers,
Lakes, Fields, and Life

DAN BROWN

BEAVER'S POND
PRESS

Da Fishi Code: Serious and Not-So-Serious Stories from da Rivers, Lakes, Fields, and Life
© 2020 by Dan Brown

Book design and typesetting by Mayfly Design
Cover image by Terri Hedrick / Solveit Studio
Managing Editor: Laurie Buss Herrmann

ISBN 13: 978-1-64343-853-5
Library of Congress Catalog Number: 2020905037
Printed in the United States of America
First Printing: 2020
24 23 22 21 20   5 4 3 2 1

BEAVER'S POND
PRESS
Beaver's Pond Press
939 Seventh Street West
Saint Paul, MN 55102
(952) 829-8818
www.BeaversPondPress.com

To order this book, visit danbrowntrout.com. Reseller discounts available.

Contact Dan Brown at danbrowntrout@msn.com for school visits, speaking engagements, book club discussions, freelance writing projects, and interviews.

To Su, my best first reader,
and to Anders and August, my favorite fishing partners

contents

introduction

If you flipped past the cover to get this far, you probably recognize my name, Dan Brown. Yes, I am Dan Brown the writer, but I am not Dan Brown *the* writer.

I don't write about disemboweled priests or an albino Opus Dei Secret Society psycho who cranks a barbed wire cilice around his upper thigh to keep thoughts of chicks at bay in order to be closer to God. First of all, that's pretty disturbing. Secondly, and I have to be honest with myself here, I'm just not smart enough to write complicated stories with intricate, twisting plots.

However, if you want to read about my experience buying a used car from a guy I suspected might be a serial killer or how my kid has outfished me since he was five years old, then this collection of stories might be your cup of tea. I've included some poignant stories, too, so I hope something in the pages of this book will appeal to a wide variety of tastes.

This is a collection of articles and stories that have appeared in various newspapers, magazines, and a couple of books over the years. Some of them are, I hope, funny, while others are a bit more serious, and perhaps moving.

A few years ago, I submitted a sample of my writings to a literary agent, and shortly thereafter, I received a phone call from a nice man who seemed somewhat confused. "You have humorous pieces in this manuscript alongside serious pieces," he said. "Your style, tone, and voice seem to be all over the map. Are you a humorous writer or a serious writer?" In response I babbled something fairly illuminating: "I'm not exactly sure what you mean. I just write, you know? My mood and what I'm writing about sort of determine how I write it." Well, needless to say, that was a short conversation. After my insightful response to his question, it seemed he couldn't get off the phone quickly enough.

I began submitting outdoor pieces to the *Chisago County Press* based in Lindstrom, Minnesota, back in 2002, covering topics such as how to catch more crappies or how to fool stream trout with a dry fly, but that sort of "hook and bullet" style of writing kept me motivated to meet deadlines for only so long. I'm an outdoor writer at heart (did I mention I have an Outdoor Writers Association of America membership card in my wallet?), but I find myself at times far more interested in writing about goofy day-to-day things I experienced and in looking at everyday life and outdoor adventures with a touch of humor. If you keep a sense of humor about you, there really is no end to what you can write.

I was fortunate with the *Chisago County Press* because the paper's owner and publisher, Matt Silver, always published what I submitted to him, and I heard that some of my funnier and heart-rending pieces garnered more attention from readers than articles about catching fish and shooting birds.

I originally had a thought to arrange the stories in this collection in some semblance of order. You know, a chapter for more serious writing and a chapter for the nonoutdoorsy silly and inane writing, but I decided to forgo that in favor of simply putting them in the book in no particular order—just as readers of my weekly column have come to expect.

Are all the pieces in this book unbelievably good? Well, did Babe Ruth swat a dinger every time he lumbered up to the plate? There you go then. Some of the stories are, I think, really good, while others are, as we say in Minnesota, pretty darn good. I withheld any stories that would give you the impression I was furiously chomping on a number two pencil or making fish lips while writing against a looming deadline. I admit to submitting more than a few clunkers to the newspaper over the years, so I will spare you the agony of reading them. You're welcome.

If you like to read and always seem to be short of time, this could very well be the perfect bathroom companion book. However, that being said, if you find yourself reading more than three or four of my stories during the course of a day, you might want to seriously consider dialing back your fiber intake.

I have given some thought to what people might say about me after I kick the bucket. I know, that sounds kind of macabre, but let's be honest, who doesn't entertain that thought on occasion, right? At my funeral, I'd be happy if someone said something like, "Yeah, let me tell you what, that guy could fish. Heard he caught a sturgeon one time on a fly rod. I guess it was like thirty-eight degrees out. Fell neck-deep into the river—*twice*—and it took him damn near an hour to land it. He was shaking so bad afterward, his kid had to drive him home. Crazy sumbich was so cold, he was blue. I don't think he made a huge impact on the world, but I think he had a book published. That's pretty cool I guess."

That being said, I'm not planning to go anywhere anytime soon. After all, I have quite a few pretty good outdoor stories that I still need to put down on paper. As for the sillier stuff I write about, I run into plenty of goofballs and craziness on a fairly frequent basis, so there truly is no end to my subject matter.

Anyway, for the sake of posterity, I thought it'd be neat to have a book on the family bookshelf with my name on the spine. Heck, if I really need to feel like a big shot, I might even slip it in next to the other Dan Brown's books.

DA FISHI CODE

Twenty-Three Incher

Last Sunday, I witnessed once again what is quickly becoming an all too familiar sight: my son Anders standing at the front of the old aluminum fishing boat, his fishing rod severely bent, battling an enormous fish.

If Anders had a few more years on him, I probably wouldn't make such a big deal out of it. But the fact of the matter is he's a twerpy eight-year-old. This makes his uncanny ability to consistently hook colossal fish—and outfish me more than I'm willing to admit—a point of considerable pride *and* annoyance.

I mean, shouldn't a kid work his way up to world-class fish? What's wrong with the tried-and-true formula of a youngster spending at least a few unproductive years on the water, like the rest of us schmucks, before hitting the proverbial jackpot?

After netting the bass and removing the hook, I snapped a few quick photos before releasing it unharmed back into the lake. I knew Anders had caught quite a smallie, so before turning the fish loose, I laid it against a rod blank and mentally marked the rod at the point where the lower jaw ended. It was about five inches beyond the stripping guide. When we got back to the cottage, I used a yardstick to measure from the top of the cork handle (where the tip of the fish's tail rested) to the stripping guide. That measurement was eighteen inches. Add about five inches to that and I'd call Anders's smallie an honest twenty-three incher.

Keep in mind, it's conceivable that many anglers will fish their entire lives without seeing a smallie that size. To put it plainly, a

Anders—aka Grasshopper—with a very large smallmouth bass caught at our family cottage in Vilas County, Wisconsin. I purposely omitted a story from this book that explains the unconventional method we use to consistently fool these fish year after year. I could tell you, but then I'd have to . . . well, you know how the old saying goes.

———————————

twenty-three-inch smallmouth is pretty rare, something akin to catching a fifty-inch muskie.

When I was growing up during the 1970s, one of my favorite old television programs was *Kung Fu*. Remember that show? Well, when it comes to fishing I like to think of myself as "Master," the groovy old white-haired blind Shaolin dude with the wall-to-wall rice paper floors and a fistful of pebbles. Anders, of course, I compare to the soft-spoken Kwai Chang Caine, or "Grasshopper," as he's known to every middle-aged person alive on planet Earth.

Every once in a while when we're out fishing, I like to turn thoughtfully to Anders and, like the Shaolin Master, lay some valuable pearls of Eastern wisdom on him. You know, just to kill time between hook-ups. I'll gently lay down my fishing rod, steeple my fingers, and say something like, "The mouth of the smallmouth bass isn't so small to the minnow that fits inside of it." After the imaginary gong quiets in my head, Anders will look at me like I'm a lunatic and reply, "Dad, why are you talking with that funny accent? That's weird. Can we just fish?"

Anyway, what I'm getting at is that an eight-year-old is way too young to snatch the pebble from the Master's hand, isn't he? And is it right for an eight-year-old to keep an accurate count of fish caught during a relaxing outing with his dad? What kind of kid reminds his pop after two hours of fishing, "I don't know if you're keeping track, but I'm up eleven to nine," and then pastes a big cheesy gap-toothed grin on his face?

Of course, I couldn't be happier for Anders. He's a wonderful partner to have in the boat and deserves every bit of good fortune that comes his way.

I'm writing this from the deck of our cottage overlooking the lake. It's another beautiful, cool morning in the Wisconsin Northwoods, and the fish are calling. We'll chase the smallmouth again today, but I don't expect to see another fish like the one we saw yesterday for quite some time.

THE iCE FiSHiNG QUiZ

"So Augie, what's the most important thing to remember when you're out ice fishing?" I ask my younger son this question every single time we prepare to venture out onto the ice. He's now six years old, and I've been asking him this question since he was two. As I wait for his response my wife jams an eternally damp pair of mittens on his hands out on the back porch.

Augie's eyes dart around the room as if looking for a clue before settling on a jumble of LEGOs lying on the floor. He closes his eyes to concentrate. He knows the answer—it never changes—but for some reason today he can't seem to come up with the right words. Augie tentatively opens one eye and gives it his best shot: "Stay awake?" The rising inflection in his voice reveals his uncertainty.

The correct answer is to stay dry. I'll accept slight variations, such as keep dry, remain dry, or be dry—as long as the word *dry* is somewhere in the answer. This may sound far-fetched, but over the past four years, Augie has never, ever stayed dry on an ice fishing trip. Never. Not one single time. Honest to God, you could turn this kid loose in the middle of the Sahara with nothing more than a couple of bent willow sticks for dowsing rods and he'd find water. Augie would find a way to get completely wet in the middle of a desert.

So we set out to go ice fishing anyway, knowing full well that, for the umpteenth time, Augie would soon become very wet and very cold. You'd think by now I'd be smart enough to take along two of everything for him—two pairs of boots, two pairs of long johns, two pairs of socks. I guess I have two pretty good reasons why I don't. First of all, I'm a guy, and that would make too much sense. Secondly, even if I had them along, I'd probably forget I had them. So Augie getting wet has simply come to mark the end of the trip. In my mind it's easier to plop the little urchin into a warm vehicle and drive home than it is to strip down a sopping wet kid and re-dress him out in the middle of a frozen lake.

Last Saturday we fished out on Chisago Lake. We heard that a guy caught about fifty crappies in the same area the night before. Naturally, we had to give it a try. My brother, Jim, drove out from Zimmerman to join Augie and me, along with my older son, Anders. We weren't there more than twenty minutes before Augie decided he should step out of the icehouse and jump up and down with both feet on a hole that had a skim of ice over it. The ice gave way, and suddenly Augie was in the hole. And very wet. The crying started before the sun dipped below the treetops, well before we caught the first crappie.

Thankfully, we did have one dry pair of insulated bib overalls. Inside the icehouse, all eyes were on Augie. Would he continue to act out and force a call to Mom on the cell phone to arrange for a pickup? He sat in a folding chair in the bib overalls, his bare feet propped up next to the propane stove. He dried his eyes and proudly announced that he could fish like that. No problem. He was good. He didn't whine. He didn't complain. He sat there and quite happily caught crappie after crappie in his bare feet. When he got tired of catching fish he stretched out on the lower bunk bed and took a snooze under a pile of jackets. We woke him up at eight o'clock after the bite slowed, but not before we had caught around eighty fish, keeping two good limits of crappies and one bonus walleye.

This particular ice fishing trip with Augie ended as many of them do. I parked the truck in back of the house and walked around to the passenger side, where I slung a limp Augie over my shoulder, his feet leading the way to the back door and a warm bed.

initiating THE uninitiated

I t's not often that I have an opportunity to introduce a new ac-
quaintance to the sport of ice fishing. Last Saturday, when I
discovered that my new fishing partner for the day was a recent
arrival from New York City (and Romania before that), I knew I
had hit the jackpot. Yes, I had the distinct pleasure to meet and
fish with my buddy's friend Adrian. His employer out East recently
transferred him to their Minneapolis office, and I felt an obligation to, as a goodwill gesture, show Adrian our unique northern
ways and customs.

I knew I couldn't completely undo Adrian's elegant and cul-
tured New York ways in the course of an afternoon. But I thought
he deserved, at the very least, a taste of spare, one-syllable conversation while he experienced the high-risk-low-reward practice of
braving the bitter cold in exchange for a few pounds of fish fillets.

To folks from other parts of the country or world, our favorite
winter pastime must seem the most foreign and crazy folly imag-
inable. On some level, they can understand the idea of drilling a
hole through the ice and silently watching a little bobber just sit
there for extended periods of time. This doesn't require too much
of a stretch of the imagination. What they do have trouble with,
initially, is the idea of driving a full-sized vehicle out onto a frozen
lake. For as often as they've heard about this odd winter custom,
none of them are mentally prepared for their first experience.

As we left Sportland Bait in Nisswa for the lake, armed with a
day's worth of minnows and wax worms, Adrian's questions about

vehicles and ice became a little more pointed. "Huh, this SUV of yours is pretty big. So, uh, what do you do, park along the shore and drag your stuff out to where we'll fish?" he asked.

I had called the shop ahead of time and was fully aware of the ice conditions on the lake we intended to fish. I also knew exactly what we were going to do once we got there, but I thought I'd give him the impression that I wasn't sure yet. "Well, I dunno," I replied, trying my best not to crack a smile. "Let's run over there, check out the lake, and we'll see how it looks." A very cryptic and worrisome response, if I must say so myself. Almost as if I'd need his input when we got there to make a well-informed decision.

We arrived at the public access, where I could clearly see a plowed road leading from the shore to some distant permanent shacks out in the middle of the lake, where we would set up my portable. I could also see that the transition from the shoreline to the ice at the bottom of the access was seamless and very smooth. Not a bump in sight. Sort of like the bottom of a roller coaster. Without missing a beat, I increased speed, pressed my head against the headrest, and yelled as we shot out onto the lake, "Well, Adrian, we'll find out pretty damn quick if they've been making any ice up here!" The truck's interior door handle nearly snapped off in Adrian's hand as the color left his face and he howled, "Dear God in heaven! Is this safe?!"

Well, of course it was safe, but I couldn't resist the opportunity to have a little fun. It seems almost sadistic to admit this, but to us native Minnesotans, an occasion like that simply cannot be missed—that look of pure, unadulterated horror frozen on the faces of the uninitiated really does swell our chests with Minnesota pride.

Adrian and I did pretty well that afternoon, catching a number of decent bluegills and crappies. It's always fun to see a guy catch a bunch of fish his first time out on the ice. As you can imagine, he's been all over the world and has seen plenty of interesting things during the course of his travels. I, on the other hand, think it's pretty exotic to travel to, say, Baudette or Fargo. So he talked about Romania and Europe and New York City, and I talked about fishing around the upper Midwest; my family; and Taylors Falls, Minnesota. He's a neat guy and we got along very well. He'd like to experience more Minnesota culture and outdoor pursuits, and I think I'm just the fellow to show him around. Next, he'd like to get out into the woods for a deer hunt. As luck and circumstances would have it, I can arrange that for him.

A BRIEF AFFAIR AND REDEMPTION ON THE NAMEKAGON RIVER

Last Saturday, I found myself standing in the waters of the famed Namekagon River, near the old logging town of Seeley, Wisconsin. Over the years, I've read many fly-fishing articles about the "Nam" and viewed stunning photos of this unique river surrounded by dense pine forests but never found a convenient opportunity to fish its upper reaches for the river's famed wild brown trout. So when I had the opportunity to meet my buddy John Weinberg for an afternoon of fishing last weekend, I knew that if I didn't run up there now, I might not get the chance again this season. John, a National Park Service ranger and longtime member of the St. Paul Fly Tiers club, makes a pilgrimage with fellow club members to the Namekagon each year and knows the river's moods and insect hatches well.

In many places the Namekagon is a relatively shallow river. Numerous eagles fly overhead, so the trout are skittish, seeking protection from the constant threat by hiding out in deeper water during the daylight hours. Around noon on Saturday, I found a deep channel underneath a narrow bridge and slipped into the river, where I quietly began to ply the deep run with a heavily weighted #12 Zug Bug under an indicator. On the second cast, my indicator was pulled sharply underwater, and I set the hook

The brown trout did not disappoint on this day spent at the famed Namekagon River in northern Wisconsin. Each trout I caught seemed to be a bit bigger than the last, a situation I certainly didn't complain too much about.

on a trout that absolutely refused to be moved off the riverbed. Our standoff was a brief affair. Far too brief, as a matter of fact. The brown trout shook the hook, and I barely had time to duck as the indicator and fly whizzed past my head to land some distance downstream. Boy, I hate like hell to lose fish, and believe me, I've lost my fair share over the years. It's downright unbearable to break off or "pop the hook" on a heavy fish that leaves me with nothing more than an aching wrist and shoulder for my troubles. I realize—deep down—that it is only fishing. I really do try to be diplomatic when things don't go my way. But the truth is the big ones I've lost always seem to swim away with a fair amount of my dignity and self-respect. Admittedly, losing a good fish can keep me up at night and haunt me for days on end.

My knees still shaking, I sat down on a rock to steady myself, ran the fly's hook point through the groove in my sharpening stone a few times, and got back to work.

Lo and behold, the third cast into this run got the attention of yet another dandy brown, and after a lengthy battle, I was able to slip the net under it. To my sheer delight, the fourth cast was very reminiscent of the third and the fifth played out just like the fourth. I had only taken nine or so casts before I'd exhausted the run and was rewarded with six brown trout, each seemingly fatter and longer than the one before.

I scrambled up the rocky bank to my vehicle, which was parked at the edge of the bridge. My shoulder and wrist were sore, but it was a good kind of sore, reminding me on the drive home of my successful first encounter with the wily brown trout of the famed Namekagon River. It's a good thing I found redemption and the trout I lost on my second cast wasn't the only good fish of the day.

Smallmouth Bass: A Scorner of Beauty and Blood

There are few things in life more exciting than seeing a fish take a dry fly on the water's surface. I realize this statement probably sounds fairly ridiculous to everyday, piscatorially challenged folks. And I'd venture a guess that anyone who *does* have the sense to agree with that testimonial enjoys fishing or, more pointedly, appreciates fly-fishing on some level.

When it comes to fly-fishing, there really is only one species of fish that'll make me all but forget about trout, particularly during the dog days of summer when insect hatches become sporadic and trout fishing can be downright frustrating at times. I'm referring to smallmouth bass, which are, pound-for-pound and without equal, the hardest-fighting freshwater fish around.

Honest to God, if smallies grew to be forty pounds, I seriously doubt we could catch them on conventional equipment with any consistency. I'm not kidding. That may sound like a stretch, but they really do fight so hard that they torture even the best equipment.

Each year, our family enjoys a two-week vacation at our cottage in extreme north-central Wisconsin. No television, no computer, and no telephone. In other words, we're totally "unplugged," and we seriously couldn't imagine a better family vacation. We walk, bike, hike the woods in search of blueberries, swim, and, of course, fish.

At the lake, my two sons and I are fortunate to catch quite a few oversize smallies with our fly rods. We locate them during the day by running large weighted buggers off our lake's deep breaks and, most fun of all, entice them with both hard-body and deer hair poppers from about 7:30 p.m. until dark. After casting a large and ungainly fly into the shallower water near the shoreline, we let it sit for a number of seconds before aggressively stripping it back to the boat. Usually, the initial plop of the fly onto the water's surface gets a smallie's undivided attention, and all it takes to elicit a vicious strike is one or two short and quick strips of the fly line, causing the fly to dive and gurgle underwater and make a loud *blooooop* sound. Let me tell you, the smallies crush those flies with a vengeance when they come to the surface.

Zane Grey wrote a short story for the May 1909 issue of *Outing Magazine* titled "The Lord of Lackawaxen Creek," where he described in detail his epic battle with an enormous smallmouth bass:

> Then I struck with all the power the tackle would stand. I felt the hook catch solidly as if in a sunken log. Swift as flashing light the bass leaped. The drops of water hissed and the leader whizzed. But the hook held. I let out one exultant yell. He did not leap again. He dashed to the right, then the left, in bursts of surprising speed . . . the speckled trout wise in their generation, the black and red-spotted little beauties keep to their brooks; for, farther down, below the rush and fall, a newcomer is lord of the stream. He is an archenemy, a scorner of beauty and blood, the wolf-jawed, red-eyed, bronze-backed black bass.

I've recited Grey's story over and over in my mind while thinking often about a particular fish that Anders and I briefly encountered out on the lake last season. After setting the hook on an unseen fish, it promptly snapped my new fly rod in two like dried kindling. I have no reason to believe that the fish in question wasn't an enormous smallmouth. It happened so quickly and the fish pulled with such brute strength that I simply didn't have time to be angry or sad or blame the rod's manufacturer—or myself for that matter. Anders looked on in wide-eyed amazement as I quietly gathered the shattered pieces in my trembling hands with as much dignity as I could muster. Together we wondered, had the rod and line not broken, whether or not I could've actually managed to land that fish.

Perhaps that fish was the size of the smallmouth bass that vividly and lucidly haunts my dreams on those nights when I shift between drowsy wakefulness and sleep: a recurring dream that is always too brief and won't allow me the satisfaction of seeing and feeling the fish in my hands. Perhaps I wasn't angry or sad when the fish got away because I already knew, somehow, the outcome of the battle before it even began.

If the definition of poetic justice is an outcome in which virtue ironically triumphs vice, well, I suppose you could say that justice was served that day. Although that certainly doesn't mean I have to like or accept it.

River Monster on a Fly Rod

Maybe I don't have the same maniacal and grizzled look as Jeremy Wade, host of Animal Planet's television show *River Monsters*, but I'm here to tell you there's no need to jet off to Ecuador or the Congo to find really big fish. Save your airfare and skip the malaria shots, because there are plenty of big fish right here in our own neck of the woods.

Last week my son Anders and I fished the Wisconsin side of the St. Croix River at Interstate State Park in hopes of landing some feisty backwater carp. The air temperature was thirty-eight degrees, with a strong wind and ice-cold rain, so we bundled up and headed out. Armed only with a 7-weight fly rod, I hoped to tangle with something sizable. When you cast your line in a river, you just never know what could be lurking beneath the surface.

It took about a half hour of standing in the river for it to happen: my taut line suddenly slackened and then responded with a very heavy weight pulling on the other end. I set the hook a few times for good measure, only to discover in short order that I was not going to be completely in control of the battle about to ensue. I also deduced that this was no carp. Initial efforts to turn my unseen foe were woefully inadequate.

The moment the fish was hooked, it seemed to develop a rather hasty plan that seemed completely contrary to my own, swimming at a measured and steady rate straight out into the river's fast current. Where and how far the fish intended to go I had no clue.

It took the better part of an hour and two unplanned swims to subdue this sturgeon. On that cold spring day, my oldest son, Anders, and I fished the St. Croix River in Interstate State Park, Wisconsin. What a test for a 7-weight fly rod!

But when I glanced at my reel and saw the bright orange fly line burning off the spool to quickly reveal the backing, I was a bit worried. I gave the drag knob a few more tentative clicks in the hope that the fish would, at the very least, slow down a bit.

The fight lasted fifty minutes, during which time the fly rod was bent to its limit. So much so that the rod's blank was bent right through the cork handle. I seriously wondered whether or not the 7-weight was up to the challenge. I stepped off some submerged rocks twice and was forced to swim back to where I could get my feet under me again, all the while holding the rod up and out of the water with my left hand. I was cold, and my left shoulder, arm, and wrist were close to losing the battle.

Between the strong current, submerged trees, and two un-planned swims, I really should've lost this fish any number of ways, but somehow we got it in. Anders waded out to his knees to tail the beast, pulling it up into the shallow water.

After it was all said and done, I was just about as cold as I've ever been. I had Anders drive home because I was shaking so badly. What a rush though. A fifty-inch sturgeon hooked and landed on a fly rod. I'm glad Anders and I braved the elements and got out there and fished.

In September, when the sturgeon season officially opens, I hope to hook and land an even larger fish on a fly rod. There have been reports of fish approaching seven feet. I'll be sure to use a bigger rod. Maybe a 12-weight. I want to tie into one of these fish. I want to feel its immense power and hang on for dear life. Then I will strain to hold it up for the camera with an ungoverned look of sheer excitement on my face. Yes, river monsters do exist, and they're a lot closer than you think.

COLD TOES AND RAINBOWS

B ack in March I promised my two boys that I'd take them to
Seven Pines Lodge, near Lewis, Wisconsin, to do a bit of early-
season fly-fishing for trout. Waking up that Sunday morning and
seeing the snow begin to fall and the wind pick up, I expressed my
concerns that maybe it wasn't the best day to go fishing. Anders
and August simultaneously threw their heads back and pitifully
moaned, "Awww! No fair! You said we were going to the lodge today!" Well, what was I to do? After all, I did promise them that
we'd go. If I had only myself to think about, I would've rushed out
the door to fish in a blizzard, but with a three- and seven-year-old
in tow, it had all the makings of quickly becoming the shortest trip
in recorded history.

After we arrived at the lodge and the boys jumped out of the
truck, it took Augie all of thirty seconds to somehow punch his
right boot deep into a snowbank. I grabbed him by the shoulders and attempted to extricate his leg from the hard pack. His
snow-covered foot emerged, but the boot and sock remained deep
in the snow. The tears started, and wails of "I'm cold!" and "I want
to go home!" filled the air. So it suddenly became abundantly clear
that Anders and I would be working against the clock . . . a very loud
and persistent clock named Augie.

We trudged through the snow down to the stream, where Anders and I picked up a few trout right away, taking turns catching
fish out of a good run. Then I hit a good rainbow that was easily seventeen or eighteen inches. I had Anders hold the fish for a

My youngest son, Augie, making it known in no uncertain terms that he would prefer to be at home instead of fishing for trout in a heavy blizzard at Seven Pines Lodge (Lewis, Wisconsin).

quick picture because his hands were beginning to get cold and I really didn't want him fumbling with my new camera.

Convinced there'd be another good fish there, Anders was determined to keep after that particular stretch of water, so Augie and I moseyed downstream a bit to try a different spot. By this time Augie was definitely ready to go, so I finally gave in and put him up on my shoulders, assuring him that we were mere moments away from heading back to the warm truck and home.

Then, as if right on cue, Anders began yelling for me, "I need the net! Hurry up! It's huge!" I looked through the heavy snowfall to see Anders's seven-and-a-half-foot 4-weight fly rod doubled up to the cork and throbbing under the strain of a heavy fish. He was palming the spool, and I heard that telltale sound that only a good fish makes as it burns line off a reel in a big hurry. I ran upstream with Augie bouncing and flailing on my shoulders, mad and screaming again because we suddenly changed directions and weren't heading back to the truck any longer.

Well, lo and behold, there was Anders with a dandy rainbow that he worked to the bank. After Augie's less-than-graceful dismount from my shoulders, I slipped the net under the fish, and once again, Anders, the punk seven-year-old kid, caught the big fish of the day. His rainbow taped out at just under twenty-one inches.

I know Augie would just as soon forget about that hour we spent at the lodge. His rod was rigged up, but he told me in no uncertain terms that he didn't want to fish. It's pretty hard to misconstrue a 120-decibel, earsplitting "NO!" from the boy. That was fine. Forcing a fly rod into his hand on that day, or any day for that matter, wouldn't have been the smart thing to do. As far as Anders and I were concerned, it was a magical hour on the stream. The weather conditions certainly weren't ideal to be out chasing trout, and it would've been easy enough to call off the trip from the warmth of our living room, but now I'm glad I kept my promise and we stuck with our plan. I was also proud that the kids hung in there and experienced some late-winter trout fishing.

Anders's hands were beet red by the time we quit, but he reluctantly bit off his fly and wound the line through the guides and onto the reel. On the drive home, we made plans to return to the lodge when the weather was nicer. The trout, as always, would be there and waiting for us.

Dan Brown, Fishing Private Eye

O n a dark night so late you could almost call it early, my fingers mercilessly pounded the keys on my little laptop. The keyboard was getting the workout of its life and beginning to get hot to the touch. That got me thinking about griddles and buttermilk pancakes and how long I needed to wait before I could eat breakfast, but my empty stomach would have to settle for cheap bourbon and wait its turn. I still had plenty of investigative work to do, and the clock was ticking. I was leaving for Nisswa on Friday to do some fishing, and I had to get real smart in a real big hurry.

I spent quite a bit of time that night poring over Brainerd area fishing reports and forums, looking for the straight dope on the local fishing angle. On every fishing forum, there are always a few saps logged on that give away one too many details about where and when they're catching fish. Details that prove to be quite valuable to a smart and resourceful gumshoe like me. They just can't keep their yappers shut, and it was paying off in aces for me. I was in luck. I found enough sap out there on the internet to start my own maple syrup business, which only got me thinking about pancakes again.

If snooping around outdoor forums and sniffing out fishing hot spots like a Bluetick Coonhound weren't bad enough, I've begun to pull the "writer card" more and more often lately.

Just the other day I phoned Sportland Bait in Nisswa, Minnesota, identifying myself as a staff columnist for *Outdoors Weekly* magazine. That statement is true enough; I do write a weekly column for that particular fish wrapper. But I wasn't being completely honest. I knew that most times, just the mere mention of the magazine will loosen the lips of the grouchiest bait shop owner. Tell the guy that you intend to write a piece about his business, the area lakes, and the terrific fishing opportunities that await the multitude of readers, and he'll really open his beak and sing like a canary. What's the guy gonna do? Feed me crummy information and risk equally bad press? No, when I sidle up to a bait counter wearing my trench coat and Sam Spade fedora with the glossy Outdoor Writers Association of America card tucked behind its satin ribbon, believe me, their eyeballs flash dollar signs and begin to spin like a one-armed bandit. They all know good press brings business.

The deal closer is the moment I whip out my little spiral notepad, pull the stubby number two pencil from behind my ear, and ask them to spell their name—you know, for accuracy. I surely wouldn't want the guy's name misspelled in print. "Bob, you say? Just Bob? B-O-B? Got it." After that, let's just say that the only question left for me is, "How many big fish am I going to catch that day?"

Do I believe that trolling the internet and pimping magazine inches for fishing information are shameful and cheap ways to find fish? Oh, absolutely. There's no doubt about that. Do I lose any sleep over it? All I'll say to that is I wake up every morning feeling well rested and quite refreshed.

It's a dog-eat-dog world out there. The competition is stiff and business secrets are well guarded, even in the fishing world. I do take pride in the fact that I'm getting pretty slick at finding good fishing spots using very questionable tactics.

Sometimes I think I missed my calling in life, particularly after I've cracked some wise guy's code on a forum or triangulated a great fishing spot using a number of seemingly unrelated reports. Maybe the world is short one really good detective or private eye. I guess we'll never know.

USED CARS: A LEAP OF FAITH

D o you know what makes me nervous? Buying a used car makes me very nervous. I'm sure many of you out there have been in the pickle my wife and I were in this past week. Your piece-of-crap vehicle gives up the proverbial ghost, and you find yourself · desperately searching used-car ads online.

First of all, I have to mention that we set a five-thousand-dollar spending limit on ourselves. To be perfectly honest, that's about all we can afford, so right from the get-go we had one or two strikes against us. Have you purchased a used vehicle lately? Any idea what five thousand dollars will buy? Let me tell you, it ain't much. One guy on Craigslist had (according to the subject line) a late-model Ford Focus advertised for three thousand dollars. When I clicked on the ad, I saw a car that looked like it had been driven eighty miles per hour into an immovable object—maybe a brick wall or something of that nature. He wrote in the description that it needed some front-end work. You don't say.

So last weekend Su and I found ourselves in dire straits. The carousel of life would mercilessly fire up again on Monday, with one son needing to get to a baseball game, while the other son had to be chauffeured to karate. Time was running out, and we could almost hear the hiss of compressed air and the calliope music begin. We had to find something halfway decent and we had to find it quickly.

On Friday, I saw an ad on Craigslist for a 2002 Saturn sedan: "Runs and drives like new—$3,800." I clicked on it and saw what looked like a new car. Not a mark on it. When I called the seller, he reported that two other guys were on their way up to Forest Lake from the Twin Cities to see it. He also said that the first one there to look at the car had first dibs, so I called Su right away and had her pick me up from work.

When we arrived at the Walmart parking lot where the car was parked, we couldn't believe what sat there in front of us. The car really did look new, and the interior proved to be in even better shape than the near-perfect exterior.

Then the seller showed up. He had a nervous look about him when he admitted that he was in the business of finding cars in need of a bit of work, fixing them up, and then selling them. Oh boy, here we go. Of course I asked him what kind of work he performed on this particular car. "Well," he said, "I think someone must've driven this car into a ditch or something. Both front airbags deployed, but there wasn't any damage to the car." Call me cynical, but the term "immaculate deception" came to mind. Despite wearing my best thrift store duds, I slid under the front end of the car to have a look around. I didn't know what I was looking for, but I do know what duct tape and bailing wire look like. It was clean. The car even looked new from the underside.

The last thing that struck me as a little funny before I haltingly handed over the cashier's check was the seller's middle name—Wayne—printed on the car's title card. He had one of those three-name names that sound pretty ominous when you say it out loud. Did you know that more serial killers share the middle name Wayne than any other name? Naturally I thought of John Wayne Gacy and almost asked him if he did any part-time clown work at local church events. I mean, the car was too clean, you know? I popped the trunk one last time and scanned the flawless interior for an errant hair or suspicious stain. Maybe I should've quickly run into Walmart and bought a UV black light and a box of latex gloves. Where's a good CSI kit when you need one?

Well, you can't put toothpaste back in the tube, as they say. The car is ours now, and three days later, as advertised, it still runs and drives like new.

Yesterday I slipped an old George Jones CD into the slot on the car's dash. I thought it would be fitting if I were listening to the mournful strains of "A Day in the Life of a Fool" when the car's engine blew and a bright red idiot light on the dash flashed "Sucker!" I figure misery loves company, and George Jones is indeed fine company, but that light didn't flash. I guess only time will tell.

one-track Fishing mind stumps scientific world

They say a typical man thinks about you-know-what every seven seconds. Personally, I find that hard to believe. That'd leave a guy like me no time during the day to think about fishing. However, if the findings of that obscure study are true, I think I have some reason to be concerned.

Each year about this time I begin to seriously think about trout fishing. By serious I mean frequent, invasive thoughts of me on a quiet stream surrounded by lush green foliage under a golden sun and a clear azure sky. I suppose I begin to think so often about stream fishing this time of year for precisely that reason. It's the season. The season of long nights and short days. Bright sunny days that look deceptively warm—until you see the mercury on the outside thermometer, stuck near the twenty-below-zero mark, telling you otherwise. It's the season itself that carries my mind away to open water, and the feeling of the sun's rays warming the back of my neck and hands. Actually, it's a pretty effective coping mechanism that sees me through many bitterly cold days.

Of course, maybe it's simply the case that I'm not quite wired right. Maybe my one-track fishing brain would completely set the psychological world on its ear. In my overactive imagination, I have a cartoon bubble of a tweedy, pipe-smoking German psychoanalyst giving a lecture at Princeton to an auditorium full of grad students. An overhead projector shows an image of me on a screen wearing canvas waders and holding a fly rod. My eyes look distant and unfocused. Mr. Tweedy taps his lectern with a wooden pointer and begins to address the audience in a thick German accent. "We've conducted extensive dream analysis and interpretations on this particular individual and found that his frequent dreams of fishing mean absolutely nothing more than fishing. We found him completely devoid of dream symbols and latent ideas representing repressed emotions and drives. Hmm. Very interesting indeed. There doesn't seem to be a single clear thought in this man's head—conscious, unconscious, or otherwise—except fishing. A pity really."

So the next time you engage me in conversation and get the uneasy feeling I'm staring at something a half mile behind you, don't panic. You're not losing your marbles. I'm simply tuning you out. Along with whatever nonsense you're attempting to tell me. Don't take it personally. I'm just thinking about you-know-what. And now that you know my you-know-what doesn't mean what you think it means, you can breathe a bit easier.

Oh, one last thing. If I break out in a broad smile while you're droning on and on, it has nothing to do with the content of your one-sided conversation. I'm smiling because I just slipped my landing net under a beautiful brown trout.

I'm sorry, would you mind repeating that? I didn't catch what you just said.

Flea Markets: A Completely Different World

I spent a couple of hours on Sunday at a nearby flea market in St. Croix Falls, Wisconsin, and discovered I had the makings of a pretty good piece. All of the wonderfully weird and eclectic things I was hearing and seeing while I was there overwhelmed me, and at one point I actually asked a vendor if he had an extra pen and piece of scratch paper handy so I could take some notes.

I assume most of you have been to a flea market. If you're as interested in diverse human behavior as I am, you soon realize that a typical flea market is sort of a strange place and that hardcore, seasoned vendors seem to be stamped from a particular mold.

There is a fairly uniform look to the vendors, particularly the men. If you have a proclivity for sweat-stained straw cowboy hats, checkered short-sleeved western shirts, and very large belt buckles, you'd almost have the look nailed. To really look legit though, you need to maintain your weight at around a buck twenty and have a non-filtered heater hanging off your lower lip. You get bonus points if you can somehow keep the cigarette ash between two and three inches in length as it bobs precariously up and down while you're talking. The only thing that might beat a long heater ash would be a personal mobility scooter (with the wire basket up front) parked behind the vendor's tent.

The first place I popped into last Sunday was a wood-framed walk-in structure run by an older couple. I'll tell you what: these folks had a very serious Elvis thing going on. I mean really big. So big that they sold framed copies of newspaper clippings announcing Elvis's death. And if that weren't creepy enough, they also sold laminated photocopies of the Nashville medical examiner's report. Not to mention lots and lots of knives and various edged weaponry, so I ducked out of there while the ducking was good.

I then spied a really nifty family-sized tent for sale a few booths down. The vendor only wanted ten dollars for it. I took a better look at the price tag and read that the poles and stakes were missing. Hmm, without poles to "tent" the fabric, can you really call it a tent? I got to thinking that if a guy wanted to spend a month or two fashioning long saplings into tent poles he might have himself a pretty good deal there. I quickly dismissed the thought, as I personally don't have that sort of time or whittling expertise.

If you decide to stroll around a flea market, let me give you some free advice. I've been poking around flea markets and dickering with vendors for a lot of years, and my nugget of wisdom is this: no matter what junk you intend to purchase, if you ask the seller what it'll cost, he'll invariably spin a very questionable tale about the junk's esteemed provenance. Some of these guys have pretty creative imaginations, so be on guard for a story like this one: "That there is a very rare harp. I pulled it out of an estate sale just last week where it sat in some old lady's living room for like seventy years. She died two years ago right there in that very house and nobody discovered her missing for well over a year. God rest her soul. Place smelled awful. That's why I got such a good deal on it, and I want to pass my good fortune on to you. I'll let that harp go for ninety-five dollars. I might be able to get a bit more for it, but there are a few strings missing and it's badly out of tune."

Another thing to look out for are the vendors who become an instant authority on whatever piece of their shit you bring to them for a price quote. I rummaged through a box of busted-up cameras and discovered an old 8 x 30 monocular that was sort of neat.

When I brought it to the vendor, he first looked through the wrong end. When I told the guy that he was looking into it backward, he quickly recovered his composure and snapped, "Don'tcha think I know that, young man? I was just making sure the roof prism mirror in there was properly aligned." He then flipped it around and focused in on some imaginary distant object and told me through clicking dentures, "Ten dollars." I could tell he hadn't been a flea market vendor for very long because the inflection of his voice rose when he said it. It sounded like he was questioning his own price. It came out, "Ten dollars?" He immediately lost my respect, so I dropped the monocular back into the box of busted stuff and walked. I didn't even acknowledge him when he yelled after me, "What'll ya give me for it?" Too late, Bobby, my interest waned and something else caught my eye.

I did discover today that professional flea market vendors and their families aren't a whole lot different than carnies or circus folks, and I certainly don't mean that in a negative way. I say that because they all lead something of a nomadic lifestyle. In a way, I can see the allure of it all. I'm a self-described antique shop and flea market junkie, so the idea of traveling around and buying and selling old stuff for a living appeals to me on many levels.

So I was running around the flea market observing things and taking notes when I happened upon one vendor who sold not only junk, but also bags of food. This guy had so much weird stuff for sale, I couldn't possibly remember it all, so I kept trolling past and, once I was out of view, taking notes. He sold caramel corn and cotton candy. He also offered up umbrellas, embroidered leather purses, nunchucks, brass knuckles, real samurai swords, and mace. I'm not talking pepper spray mace here; I'm talking a four-inch spiked steel ball attached with a chain to a big wooden stick that would have been used to bash in an enemy's head in the Middle Ages. He was closing a deal with a very young customer. "OK, kid, let's see what you got here. That's four dollars and fifty cents for the caramel corn and, let's see here, twenty bucks for the three-foot sword."

As the youngster walked away munching his popcorn with the sword tucked under his arm, the vendor yelled after him, "Don't eat too much of that corn all at once now, ya hear? You could choke!"

I do love poking around flea markets in hopes of finding an underpriced treasure. I've had pretty good luck in the past, snagging a German-made Gischard wood-and-brass barometer (circa 1920) and a pre-WWII German "Munich Child" beer stein for five bucks each. I'd put a value of a couple hundred dollars on those two items, so it does sometimes pay to have a good look at what's out on those tables. Of course, you do have to know what to look for.

If you haven't been to a flea market in a while, run out to one and do some treasure hunting. You might luck out and find some really neat stuff. And you'll likely run across some very interesting characters while you're there.

A FISH STORY FOR THE AGES

When you're a kid, it can be tough when you discover that things aren't always what they seem to be. Santa Claus and the Tooth Fairy are two prime examples that come to mind.

This past Memorial Day, my niece and nephew, Anna and Duncan, son Anders, and brothers-in-law Bil and Mark witnessed Yours Truly exhibit extreme maladaptive behavior after losing what might have been my largest walleye to date. Now, as I think back on the episode, I do believe I exhibited classic symptoms of what psychologists refer to as intermittent explosive disorder. This is not good news for a guy who recently learned he has high blood pressure, and it certainly didn't play too well with the wide-eyed kiddies.

The whole tragic episode began on Trout Lake near Boulder Junction, Wisconsin. We started fishing at nine o'clock in the morning with a plan to return to the cottage before lunchtime. Bil and I had put a few walleyes on ice the day before, so we made this abbreviated trip in hopes of adding enough fish to the live well to feed all fifteen of us staying at the cottage. Bil picked up a dandy twenty-two-incher and my son hit a good sixteen-inch eater, so things were looking pretty good by about eleven o'clock.

At eleven thirty, with the end of our fishing time plainly in sight, my pink three-quarter-ounce Fire-Ball Jig tipped with an oversize shiner was mercilessly pounded thirty feet down as we drifted the inside curve of a windswept island reef. I was spooled with PowerPro and ran five feet of 8-pound fluorocarbon leader connected by a barrel swivel. So much for the technical BS. What is important to know is that I thought I had a big walleye on the end of my line. When it surfaced we got a good look at its sheer girth and length.

After that, my memory fails me. It's all a blur. I have some hazy recollections of Uncle Bil firing up the big engine, waves splashing over the stern as I attempted to get more line on my reel, and a skinny kid working a six-foot-long net. The whole scene was very reminiscent of the movie *Jaws*. It's too late now, but what I should've done was toss a couple of classic Quint lines over my shoulder as I gallantly fought that fish. "Yeah, that's real fine expensive gear you brought out here, Mr. Hooper! 'Course I don't know what that bastard walleye's gonna do with it . . . might eat it I suppose. Seen one eat a rockin' chair one time. Hey Chiefy, next time you just ask me which line to pull, right? Back home we got a taxidermy man. He gonna have a heart attack when he sees what I brung him!"

To a nine- or ten-year-old, the first time you witness your otherwise even-keeled uncle pretty much lose his mind can't be too different than finding a box of your own baby teeth in Mom or Dad's sock drawer. Like I said, discovering that things aren't what they seem to be can be a bit disconcerting. Of course, a box of teeth doesn't scream "Goddamn it!" when you open it and scare you half to death either. I guess that'd be one fairly big difference.

After the aforementioned skinny kid bopped that leviathan walleye in the snout and popped the hook loose, I swore like a merchant marine and rod-whipped the starboard gunwale of Uncle Bil's $35,000 Lund Pro-V into submission with my new $150 rod. I guess at some point I bit down on my right index finger pretty hard. I assume that's what happened, because after we got back to the cottage I realized my finger hurt like the dickens and I could plainly see purple impressions of my front teeth behind the first knuckle.

You're probably wondering how big that walleye was, right? After giving that question a week's time and some considerable thought, I'm going to say thirty-two or thirty-three inches. When I retell this story years from now, there's no telling how big that walleye will be. Heck, by that time it could very well have been a state record fish.

A DAY FOR THE BOOKS

Every once in a while, if all the stars align just right in the cosmos, an angler might be lucky enough to experience fishing nirvana. These occurrences are rare. They are finite periods of time on the water that defy comprehension and description in a way that makes the beneficiary blush and feel like a liar when telling of it afterward. I think it's by design that we don't experience it more often than we do, because when it does happen, you know it, and it leaves you shaking your head at the end of the day and wondering if it did in fact happen at all.

Jeremy Gubbins and I had just such a day on Knapp Creek in early March. Jeremy is a transplanted English chap and a good friend. If trout fishing were an illegal activity, the police would surely bash through his front door in Coon Rapids and haul his proper British arse directly to jail. No doubt about it. Over the past few years, we've tossed flies on various rivers and streams, and I find him to be perfect company. Like me, he's a hopeless trout addict and believes that an economy of words and relative quiet while fishing is a virtue. He and I both know that there is nothing that will ruin a perfectly good day on the water quicker than fluffy, inane conversation.

Jeremy and I arrived at Seven Pines Lodge around eleven thirty and began to rig up our rods and discuss fly patterns, techniques, and strategy. As the creek was consistent with all Midwest trout water this time of year, we knew that the fish in Knapp Creek would feed in earnest during the warmest part of the day, from one to three in the afternoon. In March and April, trout need only a fraction of a degree increase in water temperature as an excuse to strap on the feed bag, so to minimize the risk of playing our hand prematurely, we decided to save the most promising stretch of the stream (a deep section that historically held some sizable trout) for that two-hour window of time.

Huffing and puffing, we trudged our way along the stream through knee-deep snow and slipped into the water below the old wooden footbridge at the appointed hour. Jeremy had made only a few upstream casts into the current rushing under the bridge when his strike indicator slowly sank below the surface. Rearing back on his dainty 2-weight rod, he enjoyed a brief taste of what lurked below the dark surface of the water before being rewarded with a slack line—minus a fly. "Bloody hell! What happened? Maybe it was my knot." I was excited by this mishap, realizing at that moment the stars, barometer, sun, and whatever else just might be in our favor that day. I casually replied, "A really, really big trout just broke you off, bloke."

For the next ninety minutes, Jeremy and I caught more trophy-caliber trout than a couple of guys deserve to catch in perhaps a decade. I'd guess that we put ten or eleven rainbows in the net that taped out between twenty and twenty-five inches. Jeremy caught most of the big fish, and I wouldn't have had it any other way. On a number of occasions, he kindly offered to trade places in the stream and allow me to fish the current seam where he was doing all the catching, but I declined more times than not. No, I felt perfectly satisfied watching a few of those marathon fish battles unfold, and the outcomes were anything but a sure thing. Jeremy's small 2-weight rod being literally bent to the cork under the strain of a heavy fish was indeed a sight to behold. I had the distinct pleasure of taking a number of unbelievable photos of oversize trout that I might not see again for a quite some time.

A very sizable rainbow trout caught by my friend and proper British chap, Jeremy Gubbins, on Knapp Creek at Seven Pines Lodge near Lewis, Wisconsin. One of many we caught during a near-perfect ninety minutes of fly-fishing on a sunny afternoon in March. Catching really big trout in small streams and rivers is always exciting.

Every once in a while, it is highly satisfying to do more observing than actual fishing on a stream. Last Sunday, I slipped my wooden landing net under the largest trout Jeremy had ever caught, and I honestly couldn't tell you which of us was more excited.

I know there are even larger fish in that stream—a particular twenty-six-inch brown trout comes to mind—and I have an entire season ahead of me to contemplate fly patterns and strategies. Maybe I'll hit that spot again soon. And who knows, if I time it right and everything lines up just so, I just might fool that fish.

BLACK FRIDAY CLAIMS ANOTHER SHOPPER

At that ungodly time of the morning, I should've been sitting in a tree waiting for the sun to rise and a deer to appear or, at the very least, shivering uncontrollably in a duck blind somewhere. Instead, I found myself at five thirty last Friday—commonly referred to as Black Friday—sitting in my SUV in a pitch-dark parking lot at the Forest Lake Gander Mountain store. As I sat there waiting and sipping hot coffee, the AM 1500 KSTP morning crew was ridiculing shoppers like me on the radio. I didn't care. It was worth hearing that infernal alarm clock buzz at four thirty. What was I to do? The store was practically giving away deluxe upland hunting vests to people like me willing to swap some precious sleep to save a few bucks. And besides, I was determined to get one.

I discovered that a Black Friday store opening at a major outdoor retailer has its own set of social dynamics that are quite distinct and highly unusual. It's certainly unlike anything you'd expect to witness at a Walmart or Target, or most any other retailer for that matter. At one of these other stores, you'd naturally expect to see a throng of outwardly excited and enthusiastic folks bundled up against the cold and waiting for hours (quite happily, no less) outside the store in a long line. At Gander, the lot was empty until 5:55 a.m., at which time I looked north to see a seemingly never-ending stream of headlights speeding south along the frontage road of Interstate 35. It looked a lot like that scene from *Field of Dreams* when Ray Kinsella and Terence Mann watched in disbelief as thousands of vehicles wound their way to the magical Iowa baseball field. I could almost hear that guy somewhere in a nearby cornfield whispering, "Price stuff low and the sleep-deprived idiots will come."

That, by the way, was just the tip of the iceberg. Not only did these pickup-driving, camo-wearing tough-guy shoppers arrive late, but it also seemed that not a single one of them was willing to tip his hand as a too-eager shopper once he got there. Heck, even after one of the groggy store clerks unlocked the front doors, these stoic dudes remained in their trucks, their true identities protected under a veil of predawn darkness. I thought, *Well, I'm here and I'm committed to stiff-arming anyone I have to in order to get my half-priced vest.* So I shut off my truck, spritzed just a hint of Trail's End #307 behind each ear, and proudly sauntered through the unlocked doors at precisely six o'clock. Evidently, that's all the tough guys needed to see. I looked over my shoulder and saw them collectively jump down from their tall trucks and hit the asphalt like Neil Armstrong leaving the Apollo 11 capsule at Tranquility Base—except these guys weren't quite willing to recite the famous line: "That's one small step for man, one giant leap for mankind."

I got my vest, just in case you're wondering. There were two extra-larges on the rack, and I got one of them. I didn't have to karate-chop anyone in the windpipe to get it either, which was fortunate for me. I can't speak from experience, but I imagine it'd be tough to enjoy the holidays while doing hard time in the county slammer.

When it was time to check out, the young guy running the cash register asked me if I wanted the receipt thrown in the bag with my hard-won vest. I squinted my best Clint Eastwood squint, hooked a thumb in the waistband of my casual Friday slacks, and hissed through my clenched teeth, "No thanks, punk. I plan on

wearing the vest and blasting some birds the minute I leave here."
The kid looked a bit nervous as he handed over the receipt, but he
let me leave the store without alerting security.

LONG JOURNEY SOUTH

i become a bit uncomfortable at the thought of traveling south. I don't know the exact reason why, but when people talk differently and I begin to hear words like "fixin'," "y'all," and "fillin' station" creep into the local lexicon, I start to squirm inside.

I have to believe in the simple fact that there are northern people and southern people. I'm definitely a northern person, and I consider anyone with an area code south of Ames, Iowa, a southern person.

That being said, I returned home in early October from a seventeen-hundred–mile round trip adventure to Mountain Home, Arkansas, where I took—and passed, I'm quite pleased and proud to say—my Federation of Fly Fishers Certified Casting Instructor exams.

And what an adventure it was. I saw the Ozarks, fished the famed White River for trout, and now know from firsthand observation what a holler looks like. Are you aware that there's a place in the Ozarks called Booger Hollow? I can't make this stuff up, folks.

I knew my Yankee-ness was frightfully apparent down there, but never more so than when I stepped into a "fillin'" station located on Highway 5 in Baxter County, Arkansas. I had reservations to tent camp at a White River resort while I was there, so I was perusing the canned goods section of the store for supper ideas when the guy behind the counter said something. I assumed he was talking to me, as I was the only customer in the store, but I held out hope he was talking into one of those ear-mounted Blue-tooth gizmos.

The guy said, "YatdaBowShowordaRiiShow."

Holy *Deliverance*! Was he talking to me? His tone didn't rise at the end of that long, unintelligible word, so I wasn't sure if it was a statement or a question. The guy was smoking a pipe and wasn't even looking at me. Judging from the direction he was facing, it appeared he was talking to a display of Black Cat Fireworks along the back wall of the store. One thing I discovered on my trip was that folks down in Missouri and Arkansas do love their fireworks. At just about every exit along Interstate 35 south of Iowa you'll see these humongous stores called Pyroworld. That's a bit disconcerting, but hey, it's the South, and who am I to judge? I guess they like to blow shit up down there.

Anyway, back to the "fillin'" station. I didn't respond to the guy because I didn't know what the heck he said to me, or if he was talking to me at all. So he said it again, only this time louder. He even italicized what he was saying, if that's possible. "YATDABOW-SHOWORDARIISHOW?" Aha, it was a question, but I still couldn't make it out. I broke down and told him I was from Minnesota and I didn't understand . . . Ozark. He finally turned to me and gave me a look like I was something unpleasant and squishy he had just stepped in. "Are . . . you . . . at . . . the . . . Bull . . . Shoals . . . or . . . the . . . Rim . . . Shoals?" He slowed down his speech and separated each carefully enunciated word with a longer-than-necessary pause so I'd understand. Based on the way I was dressed, he assumed I was fishing and wanted to know if I was staying near one the premier fishing areas on the White River.

It took awhile, but we got through it. He silently rung up my can of beans and vegetable oil and went back to his pipe. "Hey, welcome to Arkansas. Y'all have a super day and drive safe, ya hear?!"

On a more serious note, the trip was definitely bittersweet. I went down there for one reason only, and that was to take my CCI exams. Of the twelve or so instructor candidates who made the trek to Mountain Home, the number who passed the exams was definitely in the minority. The friend I'd been practicing with for the past six months leading up to the exams did not pass. One guy I know was taking his exams for the third or fourth time, and success once again eluded him. They certainly don't give away these certifications, so I feel most fortunate to have passed. A lot of it is simply how you perform for the evaluators when it matters most.

I was exhausted after the exams concluded. I broke down my campsite the following morning and began the long eight-hundred–mile journey home. I stopped one last time for gas at a truck stop off I-35 just inside the Minnesota border. After ringing up my fuel and extra-large coffee, the lady behind the counter asked, "So, ya heading north then?"

I smiled. I understand Minnesotan and she spoke it beautifully. The lilted words were light and buoyant in the air, and they betrayed her Scandinavian heritage. It was music to my ears. "You betcha," I replied. I was happy to be home.

THE ONE THAT GOT AWAY

Last fall, with only six days remaining in the stream trout season, I headed down near Ellsworth, Wisconsin, to fish the Rush River. I drove in the light rain for most of the way and felt relieved as I turned off the wipers just south of River Falls. The weather, as far as fly-fishing goes, couldn't have been better; cool air and leaden skies usually mean—to me anyway—that fishing has the potential to be pretty good all day long.

I pulled my truck into a parking area near the starting point of a good beat, geared up, and began walking upriver along a well-worn footpath. I had been walking for only a few minutes, hitting a few short runs and pocket water that tempted me along the way, when I approached a guy sitting on a large boulder. His spinning rod was propped against a sapling that hung over the bank, and a wooden wading staff, which was tethered to his fishing vest, hung at his side, its tip moving lazily in the current downstream.

My hope was that I could get by him with a perfunctory "Hey, how ya doin'?" But when he turned to face me and I saw the beer can in one hand and a sandwich in the other, I knew I was in for a somewhat lengthy conversation. Despite the fact that I chose to go fishing alone that day (to *be* alone), after a while I found myself pulling up a rock and we shot the breeze for fifteen minutes or so. It turned out that he had a lot of interesting things to say on a number of topics, and my fifteen minutes were anything but wasted. I found the guy to be pretty engaging, if not downright poignant and philosophical, as far as crawler-slinging spin fishermen go.

A couple of hours later it happened: I hooked, fought, and ultimately lost a fish that'll haunt me for a very long time. It was far and away the largest trout I've seen in a few seasons, and it was in a hard, shallow, fast turn in the river—water that I wouldn't otherwise deem suitable for such a big fish.

The huge brown hit my #14 Hare's Ear nymph on about the twentieth drift. (If nothing else, I am persistent to a fault.) Systematically working the water, I quartered what could very well have been my last cast up into the far corner of the run, and as the indicator swept around the river's outside bend, it suddenly shot four feet upstream. *Jeez Louise!* Stunned and surprised, I instinctively stripped line and reared back, making a low hook set, and there we were, engaged in the ol' Mexican standoff, neither of us giving an inch.

It certainly didn't take long for me to realize that I wasn't going to dictate the pace or outcome of this fight. All I could do was keep the rod tip high in the air and hope that the fish didn't have an affinity for jagged rocks. I applied a little pressure, thinking I could somehow wear the fish down, but after about two minutes I was not able to put a single inch of line on the reel. Needless to say, my confidence waned with every passing second. It was a long two minutes.

My left shoulder and wrist began to burn. He eventually showed himself a few times when the pressure brought him close to the surface or he decided to do an about-face. My nine-foot 4-weight rod was severely bowed, and the 5X leader was strained to its limit. Each time I caught a glimpse of this giant, my legs began to tremble and the only words that seemed appropriate to bark aloud were "holy shit!"

After repeated attempts to move my opponent out of the swift main current and into the slower inside water, I realized the trout was struggling to reach the sanctuary of a good-size chunk of limestone lying smack-dab in the middle of the fast current. It was then that I saw, to my horror, all the green grassy crap that covered the face of the rock and hung downstream of it.

Powerless against the will and determination of this fish to ruin my perfectly pleasant day, I was forced to give a few feet of line and could only watch as the leviathan brown tucked itself into the thick grass mat. I looked up and stared hard at the now still rod tip, praying it would move and pulse again. As a last resort, I dropped the rod tip entirely, allowing the line to slacken in hopes that the brown would relax and swim from its lair on its own terms. No such luck. I added tension once more and was rewarded with the sight of my Hare's Ear nymph, covered in a sopping wad of green grassy algae, flying out of the water and landing with a splat on the rocky bank in front of my feet. I instinctively screamed a single word—it wasn't a good word—so loudly that my throat hurt afterward.

The woods were momentarily silenced as birds took wing and wildlife ran for cover. No doubt mothers pressed their hands against the ears of children six miles away on the quiet streets of Ellsworth, Wisconsin.

I do believe the outcome would've been different had that crummy rock not been there. That's the feeble line I'm force-feeding myself anyway. It's a thought that is far from convincing, and I'm reminded of the Dr. Seuss character in *What Was I Scared Of?* who stated, "I said, and said, and said those words. I said them. But I lied them."

On a happier note, I've since derived some perverse satisfaction in naming that rock "KMA" rock. If you're pretty slick with acronyms, it shouldn't take you too long to figure out what the letters stand for.

I brought a lot of fish to hand on Saturday. But the lost battle for a single fish, perhaps a fish of a lifetime, rattled around in my brain for the entire drive home. I imagine it was a curious sight for passing motorists to witness a red-faced guy muttering awful things to himself while slamming his palms against the steering wheel. Visions of that battle put me to bed that night and woke me up the following morning. I'm almost hesitant to venture a guess as to the fish's length. I put a reproduction of a twenty-four-inch brown on the living room wall a couple of seasons ago, but that Rush River brute appeared to exceed that length by a good four inches. He was a pretty fish, too, with a deep yellow belly and large spots on its flanks the size of nickels. Excuse me for a moment while I mosey into the kitchen and slam my hand repeatedly in a cupboard drawer. Honest to God, it's the only thing I can think to do that'll ease the pain.

I must admit, in my mind I had already taken the pictures and made a successful sales pitch to my wife as to where in the house we'd hang another repro long before I figured out exactly how I would land this fish. Maybe that was the deal. Maybe by indulging in those fleeting victorious thoughts I jinxed myself.

A few years ago, my son Anders affixed a little sticker to one of my aluminum rod tubes. He thought it'd look neat on there. On the sticker is a little cartoon guy in a fishing hat, his hands spread wide apart and a single tear rolling down his cheek. The caption reads, "The one that got away." I never gave that sticker a passing thought, and until that day, I hardly even noticed it was there. But when I got back to the truck and slid my fly rod into its tube, there he was.

You bet I noticed him then, and I could've sworn that miserable little bastard was smiling and mocking me.

on fish camp and friends

One good thing about a tight-knit group of friends is the fact that any one single person in the group can bring a new guy into the fold and it's a forgone conclusion that he'll be a good fit. After all, your good friends did choose to hang out with you, so you have to assume they have impeccable taste in friends, right?

Unfortunately, it doesn't always work out that way, especially when a friend of a friend of a friend becomes part of the mix. In other words, with each concentric ring that moves away from your center of friends, the greater the uncertainty. I'm not exactly sure why it shakes out that way, but it does.

I can think of a perfect example right off the top of my head. It was about twenty-three years ago when a guy, twice removed from our nucleus of friends, joined us for a weekend of trout fishing and camping in Elba, Minnesota. Elba is a quaint little town nestled between high bluffs in the Whitewater River Valley, located in the southeastern corner of the state. It is beautiful country.

Anyway, it was one of those friend-of-a-friend-of-a-friend deals, and I don't think any of us—except the friend who brought him along—would be able to recall his real name.

I think he may have attended Bemidji State University, but now I can't be sure. Doesn't matter. What I do remember is that he was quite emphatic that we call him by his self-imposed nickname, Remo. Yes, I'm referring to Remo, as in the 1985 movie *Remo Williams: The Adventure Begins*. The critics panned the movie and it didn't do well in theaters, but it did become something of a cult classic on VHS and DVD. I don't want to explain the movie's plot and characters, but you might agree, particularly if you've seen the movie, that any guy who swaggers up to you and says "Hey, pal, call me Remo" might prove to be trouble. Well, he certainly didn't fail to deliver.

His adventure began when he decided to dump about a gallon of beer down his gullet at the Mauer Brothers Tavern and plow his crappy Cutlass Supreme into the back end of a five-thousand-gallon stainless steel tanker truck parked on Main Street in Elba.

I don't care where you're from, that's never a good idea. In a sleepy little town like Elba, I have to believe the local sheriff and his band of deputies were positively giddy to get a call like that over the radio at one o'clock in the morning. I mean, Remo provided them with genuine, heavy-duty cop work. Needless to say, his adventure ended in the Winona County Jail, and he was never seen nor heard from again. Good riddance, we thought. Our goofy little ersatz Remo received some pretty bad reviews from his critics back at the campsite. In defense, our friend Steve Lazarski— the guy we figured was most responsible for Remo's actions, aside from Remo himself—could only shrug and say something like, "Jeez, I didn't know he was a drunken screwup. Who knew?"

By the way, Mauer Brothers now operates a grill and serves outstanding burger baskets. For years and years the only choices Mauer offered were frozen pizzas and pickled pigs' feet suspended in some weird liquid in big glass jars. Vinegar? Formaldehyde? When I first saw the bar owner fish out a few of those things for an old local buzzard sitting at the bar, I was pretty sure I was going to die. Holy Hannah, the things have the hooves on them and everything. Seriously though, if you do get down to Elba and find yourself in the historic Mauer Brothers Tavern, take some time and have a good look around. You'll see the state record turkey, record book bucks, and countless other critters adorning the walls. There's even a huge stuffed rattlesnake and a story to go with it that's sure to keep you on high alert as you walk through the brush and sun-bleached rocks near the river.

So there you go. Some things to consider and think about. Remember to keep your friends close to the center and cast a wary eye on any shoestring "friends" that pop into fish camp.

Oh, and be extra cautious of guys who come with their own handle. Speaking for our group, we don't need any more adventures in our fish camp, thank you very much.

Five-year-OLD OUTFishes DaD

i guess I knew it would happen sooner or later. If I were a betting man, I'd have put my money on later rather than sooner. But no matter, it happened, and it couldn't have happened to a nicer kid—my son Anders.

We ventured out on a cold Sunday morning, ignoring the chilly temperatures, to do some trout fishing on Knapp Creek, in the shadows of Seven Pines Lodge in Lewis, Wisconsin.

After we arrived and rigged up our rods, I put Anders on a stretch of riffle water that undercuts an outside bank. I told him that I was going downstream about fifty yards and would mooch my way back to him. I didn't make it nearly that far. I turned my back to him and took about eight steps when he began whooping and yelled, "I got one!" I looked over my shoulder and smiled as I saw his fly rod bend and throb under the weight and pull of a nice fish. I hadn't unhooked my fly from my rod before he was into a chunky brown trout.

Before an hour was up, we'd caught and released ten fish. The brown that he caught on his second cast took big fish honors . . . for the time being, anyway.

From the riffled waters below the lodge, we walked upstream to fish a large pool below a weir. I explained to Anders that during the months of March and April, this deep pool could harbor some impressive fish, so it goes without saying that he was excited at the prospect of catching a sizable trout. We were both catching fish at the pool when I tied into a rainbow that taped out at

My older son, Anders, with a hefty rainbow trout caught on Knapp Creek at Seven Pines Lodge near Lewis, Wisconsin. I guided there for many years, and both Anders and Augie grew up fishing this creek. Despite its diminutive size, Knapp Creek was (at the time) home to some jaw-dropping trout. This photo of Anders is a harbinger of his (as well as Brother Augie's) future in the sport of fly-fishing. They were catching big fish at a young age.

seventeen inches. I felt sort of bad and made quick work of releasing the fish—without fanfare—as Anders watched with a pitiful look on his face and whined, "You *always* get the big ones . . . I *never* catch the big ones."

So, I got out of the water and told him that the pool was his, and that I'd sit down next to a pine tree and merely watch. I crossed my fingers and hoped that he'd at least have an opportunity to tangle with a good-size fish.

Then it happened. His indicator dunked under the water and he set the hook, just as he would when a trout of any size takes a nymph into its mouth. On this occasion, though, Anders could only wonder at his efforts to subdue the fish and bring it closer to him, which were useless. He looked up at his severely bent fly rod and then looked to me for help. For the second time in six months, I told him, "Hey, I'm just the guy with the net. It's your fish to catch or lose. Take your time. I'll slip the net under him when you're ready."

And so it went.

The tug-of-war continued for quite some time, and the big trout wore out his arm, but he kept the rod tip low and put line back on the reel when he could and let the fish run and tire against the drag when necessary.

When I couldn't fit the entire fish in the landing net I realized just how large this trout was—perhaps twenty-four inches. I hadn't seen a trout that large come out of a stream around here in quite a while.

Yes, Anders is quite the fisherman. Watching him cast a fly or battle a hooked fish, I need to constantly remind myself of his age and that anything less than positive reinforcement and encouragement from me could undo what will, no doubt, be a lifetime of enjoyment and success for him.

Thawing out and getting sleepy on the ride back home in the truck, Anders asked me, "So, who got the biggest fish?" It was a pleasure to reply, "You did, buddy. Wow, that was a great fish. Aren't you glad now that I didn't help you?"

A Small Cabin in the Woods

This past weekend I stayed at my friend's new lake place on the shore of Leech Lake in northern Minnesota. What makes this cabin a bit unique and endearing is its size—or, to put it more precisely, its lack of size.

There is a story about what led Paul and his wife, Patty, to build such a simple and sparse cabin on their property, but I'm afraid I might not be able to tell it as accurately as I might hope. What I do know is that originally there was a two-year plan to build a fairly large timber-frame cabin on the property. The arduous process of entertaining bids for construction, meeting with custom builders and contractors, and studying blueprints was replaced by the notion—perhaps it was an epiphany of sorts—that things could be accomplished much more quickly on a smaller and less complicated scale.

A number of things about this cabin and the property that surrounds it immediately appeal to me. When looking at this parcel of land from the lake or road, there is little evidence that the land is inhabited at all. The cabin itself is there, of course, but the large pine trees remain undisturbed and stand shoulder to shoulder like towering sentries guarding a well-kept secret. And although the cabin isn't far from the shoreline, you'd almost have to know the cabin was there to see it from the water. Even the two-track driveway leading from the road to the cabin is simple and inconspicuous by design. It's just wide enough to allow a vehicle to pass,

Paul and Patty Bury's small cabin on the shore of Leech Lake, Minnesota. Standing inside the door of the cabin and looking toward the lake, I was reminded of Thoreau's view of Walden Pond.

---

and in a few spots there are a scant few inches separating side mirrors from trees.

More important than the simple structure itself was the way it made me feel while I was staying there. The uncomplicated and functional design of the cabin makes you aware of the fact that there really are but a few essentials in life that we truly need to be fulfilled and content. Close family and friends, good books, spirituality, and nature go a long way toward preventing us from wanting those things in life that are nonessential.

After the first shafts of morning light woke me on Sunday, I put a match to the propane heater, gas lamp, and single-burner stove. As the percolator began to bubble and the smell of fresh coffee filled the air inside the cabin, I sat at the kitchen table to read a field guide to trees. After the coffee darkened considerably in the pot, I filled a cup and made my way to the lake. Under a slight breeze the inch or so of ice in the middle of Agency Narrows was beginning to move and break, making popping and cracking sounds.

On that morning it occurred to me that Paul and Patty's small cabin in the woods, with the lake a short distance from the front door and towering pines all around, felt altogether familiar. I had the sense that I'd read about such a place at one time or another in a book. The story, of course, is *Walden; or, Life in the Woods*, written in 1854 by Henry David Thoreau.

The similarities were really quite striking. Thoreau wrote of visitors to his simple one-room cabin on the shore of Walden Pond:

> I had three chairs in my house; one for solitude, two for friendship, three for society. When visitors came in larger and unexpected numbers there was but the third chair for them all, but they generally economized the room by standing up . . . My "best" room, however, my withdrawing room, always ready for company, on whose carpet the sun rarely fell, was the pine wood behind my house.

When I got home to Taylors Falls on Sunday evening, I felt compelled to rummage through the basement in search of my pocket edition of *Walden*. It's a book that has accompanied me on a number of fishing, hunting, and camping trips over the years. After finding it, I sat in the living room and turned the pages. Reading the passages comforted me in much the same way as that little cabin along the shore of Leech Lake.

Paul commented on more than one occasion that he couldn't think of a single project that he and his family completed that wasn't far more difficult and time consuming than originally planned. Woodcutting, stonework, and simple construction projects all commanded quite a bit of sweat equity. I found another parallel in Thoreau's book when I read about the construction of his cabin on Walden Pond:

> I was pleased to see my work rising so square and solid by degrees, and reflected, that, if it proceeded slowly, it was calculated to endure a long time.

I found Thoreau's words and simple philosophy of life in the woods to be just as relevant and inspiring today. There is much to be said about living a life that is simple and frugal.

One of my favorite passages in Walden reads,

> Fishermen, hunters, woodchoppers, and others, spending their lives in the fields and woods, in a peculiar sense a part of Nature themselves, are often in a more favorable mood for observing her, in the intervals of their pursuits, than philosophers or poets even, who approach her with expectation.

A small cabin in the woods on the shore of a lake is a fine place to think, observe nature, and enjoy the company of close family and friends. Paul and Patty's new place has the same centering effect on the soul as Thoreau's words and the little cabin on the shore of Walden Pond.

good reasons to go fishing

Listening to the water spill over the rocks beneath the old wooden footbridge, I feel the early April sun warm my hands and face and I'm once again reminded why fly-fishing in a river holds a special place in my heart.

Standing in the cold spring-fed water, I feel its weight press the fabric of my waders against my legs and look back to see it curl downstream. Life's single strand is now threaded through me, connecting me with the sky and water and the life beneath its surface. I am positioned downstream of feeding fish and they are unaware of my presence as I watch a smaller trout move sideways in the current to sample a bug. A pleasant sensation lingers inside me before it moves on. It is a feeling that visits me from time to time when I am quiet and still with nature. It is a consciousness, a heightened and profound awareness that I am an integral part of nature and the natural order of things.

The silence and stillness is interrupted by the sound of the drag clicking as I pull line from my reel. After making a few false casts overhead to establish distance, the small #16 olive-green caddis nymph and strike indicator dimple the water gently at the base of the footbridge. The fly's downstream progress is suddenly interrupted as the indicator hastily disappears and I instinctively raise the rod. I have every intention of stripping the line and my unseen quarry toward me, but it takes only a fleeting moment to feel the fish's power and size and realize that we have far different plans in store for one another.

It is always nerve-racking when others are watching you fish and they expect exciting things to happen. I lucked out with this large rainbow. While the guys doing the filming that day thought it was impressive to catch such a fish on a moment's notice, I knew full well there was a fair measure of luck involved. I didn't let them know that though.

I'm using a light leader—perhaps too fine—and it takes some finesse and effort to raise the stubborn trout from the stream-bed and turn its head downstream. When I first glimpse the fish broadside near the water's surface and see its deep flanks and bright iridescent markings, I'm shocked at its sheer size and yell something incomprehensible.

There are times that you lose a fish that you never have an opportunity to see, playing it briefly before the line slackens. Losing unseen fish I can take. But I saw this fish, and it would've been heartbreaking to lose it after I'd clearly gained the upper hand and begun to control the outcome of the fight. When the fish spied the waiting net, turned tail, and put on one last burst of speed, vivid images of an oversize trout I lost last fall on the Rush River near Ellsworth, Wisconsin, raced through my mind.

But this fish did not get away. I was able to experience the satisfaction of briefly holding and admiring this powerful rainbow trout in my hands before slipping it back into the water unharmed. On this day, a friend who works for an outdoor publication burned the memories of those rare moments on video and film.

Viewing the footage later, I was surprised and somewhat ashamed to watch myself behave like a fool who had seemingly never caught a large fish before. It was a moment of unbridled joy and behavior that you might expect from a young boy, not a grown man.

There are precious few things we engage in as adults that can instantly transport us back in time to our childhood and allow us to look upon the world once again with wonder. Fishing and the thrill of hooking fish do that to me. With a fly rod in my hand, I'm free to experience a peace of mind and a oneness with nature, to do only that which is necessary to fool fish in the here and now, in a particular time and space. Thoughts of yesterday or what may or may not happen tomorrow evaporate and cease to exist.

Leonardo da Vinci once wrote: "In rivers, the water that you touch is the last of what has passed and the first of that which comes; so with present time." To live life honestly, without regrets about the past or worries about the future, each of us must immerse and surrender ourselves wholly in the present.

For me, that magical experience of wonder takes place each and every time I take up my fly rod and step into a river.

A GOOD DAY TO CALL IT QUITS

I was fortunate recently to spend a memorable afternoon instructing and guiding two physicians from Mississippi on Knapp Creek at Seven Pines Lodge, near Lewis, Wisconsin. It's both challenging and rewarding to teach others to cast with a fly rod, to read the water and identify likely trout lies, and to know some basic streamside entomology in a limited amount of time.

Unfortunately, most people have a misconception that fly casting and the art of fishing with a fly rod is just too tricky to figure out in a short period. It's usually the case that folks who've never picked up a fly rod find it nearly inconceivable that they have any shot whatsoever of actually catching a trout their first time out, let alone casting a fly with any measure of grace or elegance. My job, and I'm always delighted to do it, is to demystify this sport and dispel the prevailing myths that unjustifiably shroud fly-fishing.

Well, the two Mississippi doctors, newly baptized trout anglers purified in the cold spring waters of Knapp Creek, genuinely surprised themselves that day. After forty-five minutes of instruction, their casting improved from downright awful and positively dangerous to consistently good. These guys were attentive and determined to do as well as they could, and their single-mindedness paid off in spades at the end of the day. I sometimes prefer that clients have no prior experience with a fly rod, as there is a lot to be said for not having to undo bad habits.

The fishing that day was wonderful, the weather ideal (leaden skies threatening rain that never came). The cooperative trout kept the young doctors busy with numerous hook-ups, landed fish, and plenty of streamside photo opportunities.

As an instructor and guide, I keep my fly rod with me at all times, even on the stream, but I use it only for casting demonstrations and as a nine-foot pointer: "Put your fly right there, between that rock and the far bank." As many times as I've been tempted in the past, fishing while guiding others is, in my book, prohibited. You'll understand when I tell you that it's sometimes pretty tough to watch other folks catching fish and whooping it up while your hands are tied, so to speak. My casting hand always begins to itch something fierce at about the three-hour mark, so after our time was up, I asked the guys if it'd be OK if I were to take a few casts and work a couple of fresh runs with them. We spent another half hour or so fishing together off the clock, no longer bound by the rules that govern a guide and his clients. With shadows growing increasingly longer and their dinner reservations at the lodge looming, we broke down our gear and exchanged all the pleasantries, thank-yous, and way-to-gos you'd expect to hear after a successful few hours on the stream.

Make no mistake about it, I've had guiding jobs that didn't go nearly as well as the gig with the doctors. For various reasons (some that remain a mystery to me) the stream, on occasion, is just off and reluctant to give up fish, or a client simply lacks the particular gene in his DNA strand necessary to fly cast, rendering him quite incapable of simply waving a fly rod back and forth through the air. You laugh, but I've been with folks who had hitches in their cast big enough to pull a covered wagon, and try as I might, I was simply unable to correct these problems with all the experience, patience, and encouragement I could muster. I've long since stopped being too hard on myself when things don't go as planned, and I concede that sometimes I guess it's just not meant to be.

Other days, I spend quite a bit of time untangling leaders and tippets that more closely resemble a first grader's macramé project. Don't get me wrong, I appreciate decorative knotting as much as the next guy, but a hopelessly tangled 6X leader is another matter entirely. Boy oh boy, if I had a nickel for every time I heard clients say, "Wow, you must be a very patient person to do this." On its face, the comment isn't nearly as funny to me as the delivery, which is invariably offered with a slow headshake and what I assume to be a mixture of genuine wonder and pity in their eyes. I smile reassuringly as I work at picking a snarled knot loose and tell them that it's really not a big deal. Their faces brighten, and they're always happy and relieved to hear that even experienced anglers make a mess of their leader from time to time.

Fortunately, my guiding season ended on a high note that Saturday in late September, free of hitches and tangled leaders. As I drove home in the evening I thought of the pleasant day and the smiling Mississippi doctors with their infectious southern drawls, proudly holding colorful trout for the camera. Perhaps they'll return home and tell their friends that fly casting and catching stream trout is a snap—a walk in the park. I hope they do. They were good students and did a fine job. Sometimes, it can be as easy as that if everything goes right and the trout are eager to bite. Of course, those are some big ifs, and there are plenty of them, but it does work out that way quite often.

Unknowingly, the good doctors experienced a near-perfect initiation into the world of fly-fishing, and I'm pleased when I think back on that day. It was a good day to call it quits for the season.

ALONE WITH MY THOUGHTS ON THE WILLOW

Last Saturday, I ventured down to the Willow River, north of Hudson, Wisconsin, for the opening day of the early stream trout season. This has become something of a perennial habit for me, I suppose because this river is fairly close to home, and, if the fishing is crummy, it makes for a quick return trip. Following the long winter break, I looked forward to the opportunity to once again feel a well-timed cast and a feisty trout pulling against my fly rod in the swift current.

Late in the morning, singing along to a Gordon Lightfoot CD as I wound the truck down Trout Brook Road into the river valley, I noticed several vehicles parked at the two bridges that span the Willow and Willow Race Branches. Past experience led me to believe that most—if not all—of these fly anglers would choose to begin fishing at these bridges and work their way upstream from there, no doubt due to impatience and their excitement to get into the water as soon as possible.

I chose to walk a distance downstream of the bridges, cutting through the woods and putting in below the confluence of the two branches, where I began to work my way back to my vehicle. At some point during my walk, for no other reason than to keep my mind occupied, I had the ridiculous idea that delaying my gratification would somehow appease the Fishing Gods and bring me good luck that day. I also felt foolish after laughing out

Sometimes the very best fishing—and most enduring memories—takes place when you work a river quietly and are alone with your thoughts.

loud—alone in the middle of the woods—as I recalled a great quote by John Gierach, a noted fly-fishing author: "Anyone would go fishing thinking he'll catch something. It's when you go figuring you probably won't that you know you've crossed some kind of line." The exercise of fly-fishing is, more often than not, a leap of faith, and each trip marks another occasion for hope that the fish will bite.

Well, I'm happy to report that the fish did indeed bite and I caught some dandy trout on Saturday. Nearly as important as that fact, I didn't see another angler on the section of water I fished. So, without a credible witness in sight, I smiled to myself and admired a brightly colored fish—the last trout of the afternoon—before taking a quick digital photo and slipping the fish back into the current. During those four hours, I enjoyed the warmth of the sun and felt satisfied at the end of the day to realize that I'd hooked and landed perhaps eighteen hard-fighting browns.

There were some tentative plans made last week to fish with a friend or family member this past Saturday, but looking back on it now, I'm thankful these plans didn't work out. Slowly wading a river and fishing by myself, alone with only my thoughts to keep me company, I always get a strong sense that I exist as an integral part of nature. In these rare moments, I experience feelings that I cannot achieve doing anything else in this world.

THE GOOD PASTOR

i was working my Sulphur dry fly through a long riffle section upstream. My back was facing him, so he wasn't able to see the big grin on my face when he asked me, "Hey, Danny, would it be OK if an old preacher told a few dirty jokes?" When I hear that familiar question asked over the sound of trickling river water at my six o'clock position, I know I'm on the water with my good friend Pastor Ray Singleton.

"Yeah, that'd be all right, I guess. Hear any good ones lately?" That response (or some close variation) is usually my pat answer to his question. And, of course Ray knows some good ones—a lifetime of good ones that he weaves like a fine tapestry, always guaranteed to elicit involuntary spasms of laughter. Ray is one of those guys with a special joke file cabinet in his brain. It holds literally dozens and dozens of jokes that he tells with impeccable timing.

A few days ago, I met Ray and his friends Lee and Dave at our prearranged meeting spot in Hudson, Wisconsin. One benefit to guiding others is that I'm able to make some genuine, lasting friendships with clients. During the course of the past few years, I've had the pleasure of guiding Ray, his son Bryce, and Lee for trout two or three times at Seven Pines Lodge, so it was a natural progression of sorts to arrange for a trip to new and bigger water.

Ray is a good fly fisherman. I took the time on Monday to really look at his casting stroke and timing, and he is indeed an accomplished fly caster. I saw that his fly line, leader, and fly flew through the air on a level plane, unfurled crisply at the appointed spot, and dropped softly to the water. I suppose anyone who can tell an incredibly detailed joke while managing a fly rod, thirty feet of fly line, and a sharp hook without missing a beat must be pretty good.

I also realized on Monday that the more I talk with Ray, the more I notice he's a fairly complex fellow. Not complex in a difficult or confusing way. No, he's far from that. I mean complex in its truest meaning, as in multifaceted. Like a diamond or prism that sparkles when held to the light, Ray reflects and refracts a vast array of different knowledge from many angles. I'm talking eclectic stuff—from politics, the environment, spirituality, and art that he's acquired over the course of seventy years. The other day, Ray spoke in great detail about Dietrich Bonhoeffer, the German Lutheran pastor and theologian who denounced the führer and spoke out against Nazi fascism and anti-Semitism. Like I say, pretty heady stuff coming from a guy who, if you slapped a pair of bib overalls on him, would look exactly like an Iowa pig farmer. OK, to be completely fair to Ray, I'd also mention that if you threw a bow tie and tweed jacket on him, he'd look exactly like an Ivy League professor. He's one of those broad-spectrum guys who could look like just about anybody.

The first fish Ray caught was a fat seventeen-inch brown that was fooled by a bead head nymph swung underneath an overhanging tree. I joked to Ray that it was going to be downhill from there, and he shouldn't expect to hook a larger trout that evening.

The Sulphur mayflies were waning a bit by the time we fished the Rush River. The most abundant hatches of these early-June flies had occurred a week or so beforehand. Still, a good amount of them flew off the water, and we stuck plenty of our own phony flies in front of just enough biting trout to make the trip worthwhile.

When darkness fell around nine o'clock, we headed back to our trucks, where I set my fold-out aluminum camp table with deli subs, potato salad, yogurt, and good kettle chips. We were hungry and made quick work of the food. The guys were talking about getting up early the following morning and heading north to Ely for two weeks of fishing.

We settled up, parted company, and made our way out of the valley and back to Ellsworth and River Falls before crossing into Minnesota and more familiar territory.

It was about eleven o'clock as I was getting onto Highway 94 in Hudson when the joke about the schnauzer and the Czech hit me again—twice as hard the second time around. Ray and the guys were driving right behind me in Lee's Ford Escape. I wonder if they saw me laughing hysterically.

Much like Ray himself, Ray's jokes are pretty complex. The other day, his jokes were as memorable as the fishing, and laughing while fishing is a very good thing. I hope Ray and I can fish together for a long time to come.

THE ECONOMICS OF HUNTING AND FISHING

getting dressed for work this morning, I was suddenly struck by a thought. Admittedly, I don't get them very often, so when those thoughts do come around, I tend to pay attention and, at the very least, attempt to work them out to some sensible or logical conclusion. This particular idea involved some pretty heavy-duty math that would no doubt require a calculator, so I waited until I got to the office to arrive at a solution.

The big thought involved hunting and fishing and the oft-asked question, What is the actual cost—per pound—for fish and wild game?

We all know that from a strict dollars-and-cents standpoint, attempting to put fish, birds, and hoofed critters on the table to sustain your family's nutritional needs is something of a farce, right? I mean, the simple exercise of catching a few crappies for the frying pan shakes out to about ten dollars per pound after factoring in fuel costs to and from the bait shop for minnows, boat gas, and cooking oil, to name just a few basic fishing expenses.

Walleye fishing is even worse, especially if you intend to travel to productive walleye waters such as Mille Lacs or Lake Winnibigoshish. Believe me, after calculating the cost of one of those lengthy trips, you wouldn't scoff at the nine dollars per pound they get at the supermarket for walleye fillets.

Before I forget, I should mention what I eventually figured out with that calculator at the office. If I had my way—and somebody else's money, like Bill Gates's—I'd purchase small game licenses from three states. That way, I could hunt grouse here in Minnesota, as well as up near the family cottage in Arbor Vitae, Wisconsin. Oh, and let's not forget about the fantastic pheasant hunting out in South Dakota. I was reintroduced to world-class Dakota hunting last winter, and now I've developed an expensive taste for high-end lodges, five-star cuisine, and guided hunts. Also, in addition to my Minnesota resident deer license, I'll need another non-resident Wisconsin deer license again this year to bow hunt my friends' property south of St. Croix Falls. Of course, I can't forget about bow hunting and the early October antlerless firearms deer hunt here in Minnesota. Whoops, I nearly overlooked my resident fishing license and nonresident Wisconsin fishing license, trout stamps, and guide's license. Did I mention a fish house license?

After carefully punching in the correct numbers on my little calculator, I arrived at a cost of $557 for these various licenses. The actual amount was $531, but I added $26, assuming that I'll need a couple of bonus antlerless permits again this upcoming deer season.

So, what does this all mean? It means that to get my venison, fish, and fowl in line with supermarket prices, I'll need to shoot seventeen deer, four hundred grouse, a couple hundred pheasants and catch approximately eleven hundred pounds of fish.

Or, I could sell off all my fishing and hunting equipment and buy my meat and fish at Cub Foods. You'll have to excuse me for a moment while my fit of laughter subsides. No, I don't suppose selling my stuff is an option. I hope I see plenty of deer, fish, and birds out there this fall.

i Have Just the Vehicle you're Looking for

We're living in some tough economic times. The other day I heard on the radio that things haven't looked this bleak since the 1930s. With that fact in mind, I'd like to mention that if you're in the market for cheap-but-reliable transportation, I have just the van you're looking for.

Here's another thought worthy of your careful consideration: If you're the parent of a young son or daughter who is now (or soon to be) of driving age, this van could very well be *exactly* what you're looking for, and I'll tell you why.

You can rest easy at home knowing your son won't stand a snowball's chance in hell of winning the adoration of a young gal while driving—or even leaning against—this van. Oh, and the Obama/Biden and public radio stickers that adorn the back hatch are included at no extra charge. Just think of them as added insurance and additional peace of mind.

Believe me, it's not remotely possible to look cool while driving a grocery-getter. If your boy thinks a custom paint job might help, do him a big favor and tell him to hold that thought. It will only make him look more foolish. Chrome spokes? Nope. Lowered suspension? *Please*. Curb feelers? Uh-uh. There is no way to pimp this ride and achieve elegant playa status—but that's the whole idea. Listen, you can't be with your teenage son every minute of every day, and you hope he's making the right decisions when you're not around. Well, think of this van as a big forest-green testosterone negator—a guardian, so to speak. Don't worry, Junior won't get into a lick of trouble driving this rig.

"But Dad, I want a red Mustang!" Billy pleads.

"Your mom and I lost all our bread in the stock market last year. You'll drive a van and like it. By the way, there's been a change of plans. Princeton's out. You're going to Globe College of Business next fall."

"No *fair!*" whines Billy.

"Hey, life ain't fair. Get used to it, kid."

I won't even mention teenage girls. If you have a daughter in high school in need of a vehicle, she'd probably just as soon forsake driving altogether before being seen driving a van.

There are a few areas of rust on this van, but it's not like children and luggage are going to fall through gaping holes in the floorboards. The rust is localized, located primarily along the rocker panels in front of the rear wheel wells. I might be partial, but all in all, this van looks pretty darn good for the asking price.

Of course, I'm a soon-to-be forty-five-year-old who lucked out years ago when I married my wife, Su. I don't have to look cool anymore, and thank God for that. I remember being young and thinking that trying to look cool was a lot of work.

You should also know that our dog chewed on the passenger-side armrest a couple of years ago. The dog is dead now, but not as a direct result of chewing on the armrest. (You can stop dialing the SPCA and put the phone down.) It was professionally fixed (the armrest, not the dog) in just a bit under eleven seconds with duct tape. I spun the roll of tape around that armrest faster than a cowboy in a calf ropin' contest, then finished 'er off with a couple of clean half hitches . . . "DONE!" I suppose the armrest could be looked at as another plus if you're considering buying this vehicle for a young male driver. After all, nothing exudes tackiness and repels chicks quite like a vehicle held together with duct tape.

There's one more thing you should probably know before you reach for your wallet. My wife backed the van into our recycle bin at the end of the driveway—not once, but twice—in a two-week span of time last year. Considering the fact that recycling is picked up every other week, you could say Su went two for two. Very impressive. Anyway, she insisted on spending about six hours super-gluing the driver-side taillight cover back together. Do me a favor. If you wind up with this van, drive it around town for a while with the taillight the way it is. Su would appreciate it. How she managed to reassemble all four hundred pieces and accidentally create a spot-on likeness of the Virgin Mary is something just short of astonishing. It was a little unnerving the following day when a couple from Toledo, Ohio, showed up at our front door asking to see "the miraculous image." Who knows, maybe Su was an accomplished Byzantine mosaic artist in a previous life.

By the way, Republicans are more than welcome to inquire about this van. Feel free to peel off the Obama sticker and replace it with an old "Dubya" sticker if you wish. That's cool. We can all get along.

Give me a shout and we can arrange for a test-drive. Don't bring your kid along though. Drive it home and surprise him. Years from now he might appreciate your wisdom and thank you for it.

Angry Naked Campers

If you plan to boat and spend time north of Wild River State Park on the St. Croix River in the near future, I feel obligated to report that there have been strange sightings from numerous folks—including yours truly last Sunday—of naked people. That's right, you heard me. Naked people.

For the past two days when retelling this story, I received confirmation of occasional nudists on the upper St. Croix from so many sources that I felt it necessary to call Wild River State Park directly and confer with a ranger. Yes, the ranger I spoke to on the telephone burst out laughing and indeed confirmed that nude campers and canoeists have been drawn to the upper St. Croix for many years. She also added that conservation officer Brad Schultz has been dispatched on a number of occasions to investigate these sightings.

When you think of frolicking naked people skipping over Mother Nature's forest floor, you just assume that they are a peace-loving, timid sort—you know, live and let live—that sort of thing. You half expect them to peek out at you like wood nymphs from behind trees, giggle "Tee-hee!" and run away. Well, let me assure you that this was definitely not the case with Mr. and Mrs. Crabby Applepants who called the island at the mouth of Wolf Creek home last weekend.

Good friends of mine had a run-in with them a few weeks ago, and when my family and I joined those same friends for an afternoon of pontooning, swimming, and kayaking fun last Sunday, well, there they were again, in all their clothing-optional splendor and glory.

The downstream side of many good-size islands in a river will often result in a fairly long sandbar, a perfect spot to run your watercraft's bow aground and take advantage of the beach-like conditions. Some of these bars, like the one we proudly colonized, can run a few hundred feet downstream. Everything seemed perfect last Sunday when we did just that. Kevin and I had just pulled the front end of his pontoon onto the sandbar when all of a sudden, with no time to run the CliffsNotes version of "The Birds and the Bees" by the wide-eyed kiddies, a naked woman with long, nasty dark hair burst through the island's undergrowth and snarled, "We're camping here!" She even went as far as to scream, "Goddamn kids!" from deep within the island's woods following her huffy retreat. Is it really possible to be naked and crabby at the same time?

Kevin, in the presence of his wife and son, along with my wife and boys, was good enough to temper his response by replying, "That's fine. You go right ahead and camp. We're fine here. Carry on."

Now, if you're old enough to have seen the classic movie *The Blue Lagoon*, starring Brooke Shields, I'm here to tell you that what we saw looked nothing like any scene from that movie. In an effort to mentally weather the offending visual shock last Sunday, I snapped my eyes shut and concentrated on the lithe Brooke, clutching tightly to that waning adolescent memory. In 1980, I was sixteen years old and that movie made me very happy; that's all I'm going to say about it. If any of you female readers could've stood there with me last Sunday and got an eyeful of Mr. Applepants, I suppose Brooke's costar, Christopher Atkins, would've come to mind. Another miss wide of the mark. Sorry to disappoint you.

I insist that there was plenty of distance between our parties and more than enough trees and bushes on that island to peacefully accommodate two naked campers and two families well downstream of them. I'm telling you, we could've peacefully coexisted there on that island and sandbar just fine without ever having seen or heard from one another. Really.

As you can imagine, I had a very good time writing this story. Everything I wrote is true, by the way. As a matter of fact, I had to omit a few details that probably would not have made it past the editor's desk. Believe me, you're better off not knowing.

Fishing is pretty tough this time of year. Thank God there are grumpy naked people in this world. I honestly couldn't think of a thing to write about until my wife suggested, "Why don't you write about the naked people on the river yesterday, Dear. That would make a nice story." Oh yes, I'll take my inspiration any way I can get it.

CHRIS AND ME

My old friend and fishing buddy Chris Nolt arrived at our house last week. Chris moved out to Montana with his folks and sisters when he was fifteen, and he hasn't looked back too often since. The mountains and seemingly endless western skies, not to mention incredible trout fishing and elk hunting, grabbed a hold on Chris from the start, and Montana has become his home. Over the years, I've made some trips out there, and Chris has been back here a few times himself. A couple of his visits were short ones—an hour or two here and there at the Minneapolis–St. Paul International Airport between his business flight connections, when we looked at photo albums and drank coffee.

On this particular visit, Chris brought his son, Michael. The last time my wife and I saw Michael was nine years ago when he was a two-year-old toddler. He's now eleven, and it didn't take long for Michael and my son, Anders, to get along as though they'd been old chums from the start.

Over the three days, my family and I kept the boys from Montana pretty busy. The morning after he and Michael arrived, Chris and I took a daylong float trip down the Namekagon in a drift boat, fishing for smallmouth bass. The next day Michael was introduced to my in-laws' private top-secret lake, known for big sunfish, crappies, and largemouth bass.

I've been fishing this lake now for some years, and June has always proven to be the prime month for sight-casting to big bluegills and pumpkinseeds during the pre-spawn and spawning periods. By the way, I believe I held the record for the largest blue-gill to come out of that lake. A couple of weeks ago, I caught what I believed to be an unbeatable 'gill that measured eleven-and-a-half inches long with a girth of eleven inches. Well, I couldn't be happier to report that a freaky-big bluegill was caught last Friday that shattered my short-lived record, and plenty of folks were around that day to see this behemoth sunfish. Chris set the hook on a bluegill with a 4-weight fly rod that went twelve inches long and thirteen inches around. I'm guessing that it took at least three minutes to get that fish into the boat. Keep in mind now, I'm talking about a bluegill—a sunfish—a three-minute tug-of-war to land a sunfish.

As the sunlight began to fade, Chris and I started to paddle back to the shoreline to gather up the kids, fishing equipment, and the sunnies we kept for a fish fry around the firepit that evening. As our canoe slipped through the calm water, we watched Michael and Anders for a while as they swam and whooped it up, their laughter drifting over the lake. Chris laid the paddle across his lap and said, "You see that? Boy, it's neat to see our boys together like that." I couldn't help but grin as a thousand childhood memories of Chris and me flooded my head, and I replied, "Yep. It reminds me of a couple of kids I used to know."

sHaring superior's magic

I introduced my six-year-old son, Anders, to shore casting for salmon and trout on the North Shore of Lake Superior last October, and it didn't take too long for the excitement to begin.

I was casually talking to a local angler, a retired fellow named John, early on Saturday morning near the mouth of the Lester River. No more than ten minutes from the time we began fishing, Anders yelled, "I got one! I got one!" John and I could plainly see that Anders's rod was severely bent, but we didn't get too excited initially, assuming the three-quarter-ounce spoon he was casting simply hooked the lake's rocky bottom. What got our attention, though, was when the drag on Anders's reel began screaming a moment later and we saw a large Kamloops rainbow trout propel itself some distance out of the water about forty feet from shore.

Needless to say, our conversation came to an abrupt halt as I quickly grabbed the net and picked my way across the rocks to Anders's side. I'm not entirely sure which one of us was more excited. Anders did everything right; he fought the fish like a seasoned pro and was able to put line back on the reel after the "looper" took a couple of blistering runs. The fish jumped one last time—fifteen or so feet from the shoreline and a waiting net—when it shook the hook free, righted itself, and sped away for deeper water.

My heart sank.

I plopped my hind end down on a wet boulder and contemplated flinging myself into Superior's icy waters when Anders said, "Whoa, that was cool! Did you see that thing jump?!"

Young Anders doing his best to hold a large Kamloops steelhead up for a quick photo near the mouth of the Lester River along the North Shore of Lake Superior. I have to believe that trip and others like it in subsequent years developed Anders's and Augie's love for Superior's North Shore and the trout and salmon that make their way into the lake's tributaries.

Well I'll be. Sure, he was a little disappointed, but his world didn't stop spinning after he lost that fish. He was ecstatic that he was able to battle and see such a powerful and majestic fish. And I was thrilled to witness it.

Shortly after that melee, a large fish hammered the spoon I was retrieving about fifty feet out into the lake. That day I kept my 8-weight fly rod in the truck and opted for my ten-and-a-half-foot "looper" rod spooled with 6-pound test line. This meant it took some time and patience to get the fish to shore, where Anders cleanly slipped the net under the brightly colored, twenty-six-inch Kamloops trout.

Early on Sunday morning, we were fortunate to catch another large one that went twenty-eight inches. Another angler reported that only three fish were caught near the mouth of the French River on Saturday and Sunday, so I'd say that we enjoyed more than our fair share of good luck that weekend. Although Anders fished with such intensity and unwavering certainty that "we'd get 'em," I'm not so sure that luck had everything to do with our success. His resolve and determination were infectious, and I soon found myself not merely hoping for but expecting a hook-up with every cast.

Sharing my young son's excitement and seeing our North Shore adventure through his eyes reaffirmed a strong belief I hold about fishing: memories of fish are fleeting, but memories of special times spent together and shared emotions last a lifetime.

On Sunday, Anders and I watched the hazy October sun slowly rise above the lake as we sat on a craggy rock outcropping on the shore of Lake Superior. We admired a beautiful fish lying in the net between us, its chrome-silver and iridescent flanks glittering and reflecting the sun's light on a perfect morning. In that moment, everything was right with the world.

Joe's River

A good friend of mine, Joe Krznarich, has been after me for years to drive out to Merrill, Wisconsin, to fish the Prairie River. I always think of the Prairie as Joe's river. What has prevented me from making the trek to see Joe before last Saturday is the distance from Taylors Falls to Merrill. It's quite a poke out there, something like two hundred miles, so it's maybe a three-and-a-half hour drive each way. With the rivers closer to home flooding their banks from all the rain, coupled with the fact that I hadn't chased trout with the fly rod in an unacceptable amount of time, another buddy and I decided to pay Joe and his river a visit.

Joe had reported that the large March Brown and Brown Drake mayflies were coming off the water of late, so John Koch and I thought it would be a good idea to drive seven hours round trip to fish roughly the same amount of time on the Prairie. Folks, if you're a fishing junkie like John and me, and you become truly desperate to throw flies to trout, you start to rationalize that a day trip like the one we had last Saturday makes perfect sense.

When we arrived at the Prairie, John and I went downstream, while Joe headed upstream. Joe and I carried walkie-talkies, so we kept in touch and shared with each other what flies were working and so forth. It took maybe a dozen casts with my #10 orange Stimulator dry fly to catch the first five trout. All of them were colorful brook trout, their olive backs and mottled flanks reminding me once again that trout fishing holds a special place in my heart. Not a single fish was better than eight inches, but when you're trout fishing, all the fish are good fish, and it is fooling the fish with hackled feathers and hair that makes this endeavor so rewarding.

At one point I thought about switching out my fly in favor of a Brown Drake imitator, but it was tough to argue with success. Plus, I didn't have any in my box and my pride prevented me from asking for one of John's top-secret, specially tied Cap's Hair-wing Adams. The fish continued to rise and take my Stimulator throughout the day, probably at the same rate as the Cap's, so the occasion to beg John for one of his flies never materialized.

Joe's river, the Prairie River, is a good river. It is a northern freestone river that cuts through pine forests that infuse the water with tea-stained tannin. If you are a trout angler, tannin-stained water is a good thing, as you are able to get very close to the fish without alerting them to your presence. It is a healthy and clean river, which makes for prolific hatches of various mayflies, caddis flies, and stoneflies. Joe told us of a day when the white mayflies (*Ephoron leukon*) were coming off the water so thick, it was like fishing in a snowstorm. That's a hatch I'd like to see.

To my way of thinking, getting to and from good fishing water is half the fun, and the other half is the fun I have with good friends. We spent about an hour in a nearby park around midafternoon grilling burgers and drinking a few good Wisconsin beers, so the non-fishing-to-fishing time was actually a draw.

I'll tell you what though, I never have more fun or laugh harder than when I'm with Joe and John. Between the frequent hook-ups and John and I trading favorite lines from *Napoleon Dynamite* and generally cracking ourselves up silly, we probably had about as much fun as a couple of guys could have fishing.

When John pointed his finger across the river like Farmer Lyle in *Napoleon* and mumbled, "Over there beside the pigpen I found a coupla Shoshone arrowheads," I thought I would topple over into the water. Yes, I'd make the long drive to and from Joe's river again without giving it a second thought.

STONEFLIES ON THE NAMEKAGON

A friend and I met recently in Hayward, Wisconsin, with plans to fish the Namekagon River for brown trout. We had heard from a number of sources that black stoneflies were hatching and present on the river in high numbers. Emerging from winter and anxious to cast to rising fish, fly anglers need little more than a rumor of active bugs to plan a spring trip for trout.

John Koch and I go back a number of years, meeting first on a Wisconsin fly-fishing website, then as vendors selling our wares and services at the annual Great Waters Fly Fishing Expo. John's booth at the expo showcases his original woodcut relief prints. Over the years I've known John, more and more of his prints have become available on his website and at the shows, and appreciation for his art has grown rapidly.

One of his prints, titled *Sun, Moon, Stars*, a whimsical piece featuring a colorful brook trout ringed by celestial images and aquatic invertebrates, is now gracing the current cover of *Gray's Sporting Journal*. For those unfamiliar with this highly regarded publication, making the cover of *Gray's* would be akin to seeing one of your photos on the cover of *National Geographic*. It's sort of the Holy Grail for sporting artists.

Before continuing north to our final destination near the old logging town of Seeley, John and I dropped in on our friends at the Hayward Fly Fishing Company. Larry Mann and his wife, Wendy

My old friend John Koch took this neat photo of a black stonefly with me blurred in the background. John, aside from being an accomplished photographer and artist, is one of the finest fly anglers I've had the privilege to fish with over the years. And he is one funny dude, which is probably what I like best about him.

Williamson, had just opened their shop when we arrived and were happy to share good information regarding fly patterns and where we might fish that day. Surprisingly, Larry told us of an angler who had come into the shop a couple of days earlier, reporting that a Parachute Adams pattern, skittered along the water's surface, had been taking fish.

Initially, I was a bit curious as to why a standard mayfly pattern would work to effectively imitate an adult stonefly, but looking at it from a trout's underwater perspective, I could see how the larger, circular profile of the parachute hackle, when moved erratically on the surface of the water, could fairly well represent the clumsy wing beats of a stonefly attempting to deposit her eggs along the riffled stretches of a river. Also, because stoneflies are poor fliers, they're regularly blown onto the water on days with a bit of a wind, which happened to be just the sort of day we were fishing. Of course, a fly making contact with the water almost always gets a trout's undivided attention.

Don't worry if the last couple paragraphs have you scratching your head and running off to check Google for parachute hackles and stoneflies. Let me assure you that a lot of things in the natural world, particularly when it comes to fish and bugs, continually present little mysteries that keep us learning new things every season. Believe me, I was a bit confused too.

So John and I bought a few flies and other items at the shop, said our goodbyes, and set out for one of Larry's recommended spots. When we arrived, the stoneflies were there—sometimes thick in the air, landing on our clothing and hats and fishing rods. The desired riffle water was there, and so were the trout, rising and slashing at the surface for clumsy stoneflies. We did as well as we could hope to do on the oftentimes unpredictable Namekagon River. Fish took our flies often enough to make us deliriously happy, and we smiled at one another over stretches of dancing freestone river and bent fly rods.

It was a good day to be on the water again with my friend. Alliances made in the pursuit of fish are strong and enduring. Just as small black stoneflies fill the air and restore an angler's hope each spring, I look forward to the first warm days in March and April, when I can spend time on the water with friends.

First Deer Hunt

The alarm clock clanged at four in the morning, alerting my senses to the sounds and smells of frying bacon, rattling dishes, gun oil, and coffee. Despite a fitful night's sleep, I awoke feeling energized and excited; this was the morning of my first deer hunt. After years of hearing my dad and uncles tell and re-tell their hunting and deer camp stories, I was now taking part in this rite of passage, this annual fall tradition. Hearing floorboards creaking overhead and quiet activity throughout the cabin reminded me that I didn't want to be last to the breakfast table, so I dressed quickly and made my way upstairs.

I ate breakfast with my unclesTom and Joe while Dad and Uncle Dewain studied an aerial map of the Chippewa Forest, explaining to us our options and plans for the morning's hunt. I had grown accustomed to the incessant deprecating humor my uncles directed at me, so I was surprised when Dewain asked me which stand I'd like to use and why, based on the rub lines and scrapes I'd come across the weekend before while scouting the area. It occurred to me that since the time my dad and I arrived the night before, I hadn't been the source of any jokes; they had welcomed me to deer camp and I began to feel like a respected member of the group instead of a fifteen-year-old kid.

We left the cabin at five o'clock, taking two vehicles up Highway 4 to the north end of Little Sand Lake. Along the way we dropped off Joe and Tom at trailheads to trudge through the dark, snow-covered woods to their stands. Dad, Dewain, and I walked the same trail until it forked, where I received some last-minute encouragement before we exchanged good lucks and parted ways.

With a blanket of snow on the ground, it was fairly easy to follow the faint logging trail by starlight to my stand, which I reached with thirty minutes remaining until shooting time. Sitting with my rifle resting across my legs, I had time to relax and listen to the quiet woods in the minutes before dawn. I heard the cadence of distant hunters as they moved through the woods, their boots crunching the snow and leaves and snapping twigs and branches as they walked; the sharp, high-pitched squeaking of nails in cold wood as hunters climbed ladders and settled into their stands; mice scurrying through leaves and over the bark of fallen trees; and the distinct, low hoot of owls searching for the mice.

As the sun neared the horizon, I heard the faint sound of something heavy moving through the woods, a sound unlike the rhythmic strides of a walking hunter. I checked my watch and was surprised to discover that only a few minutes remained until shooting time. Through the woods, I could see Dewain sitting very still, looking down at the trail that eventually wound its way to my stand. A few minutes later he waved his red cap high over his head, and I could only assume that a deer was heading in my direction. In the half-light of dawn, I saw the large deer fifty yards down the trail and closing ground quickly. Quietly, slowly, I shouldered my rifle, eased the safety off, and watched the mature buck through the gun's open sights as he neared my stand. I forced myself to breathe, certain the deer could hear my heart beating as I waited for the buck to quarter away; the gun roared, the report echoing through the woods until the air fell silent again.

It was a number of years later that Uncle Dewain admitted to me that, yes, that deer, my first deer, passed directly in front of him only minutes before my historic shot. When I asked him why he did that, he smiled and replied, "Danny, we all knew how excited you were that day, and I guessed that buck would stay on the trail until he reached your stand. I watched you through my field glasses, and I gotta say, it took nerve and patience to wait as long as you did for that shot. That was a great first deer."

It's been many years now since that memorable weekend. It took some time and reflection to understand why my uncles treated me with courtesy and something approaching reverence. For those three days, they recalled old emotions and saw again their first deer hunt through my eyes: they wanted my first deer hunting experience to be perfect.

A SOUTH DaKOTa PHeasanT HunT TO ReMeMBer

I'm naturally skeptical when it comes to reading sporting travel advertisements. You see them bunched up on the last few pages of glossy outdoor publications, promising fishing or hunting trips of a lifetime: "Trout as long as your leg," or "Coveys of birds so thick they eclipse the sun." If you do plan a trip to one of these high-end destinations and have enough time before you actually leave, your imagination and exaggerated expectations can really set you up for a letdown of epic proportions. After all, who can really claim to dictate the actions and behaviors of wild fish and game with any certainty on any given day?

My father-in-law and I just returned from such a trip out near Miller, South Dakota, where we joined a dozen other hunters at Dakota Wild Wings Lodge for a day and a half of pheasant hunting on twenty-six hundred acres of preserve land. Ron and I didn't want to jinx this trip, but prior to leaving for the lodge, we were both guilty of visiting their website fairly regularly to contemplate the colorful photos, most of which included piles of roosters and groups of deliriously happy looking hunters. The lodge's lofty claims of "world-class pheasant hunting" and "the finest pheasant hunting ground in North America" did indeed conjure up in my mind all of the ingredients for a hunting trip of a lifetime. Who wouldn't arrive at that conclusion? After all, that is the point of eye-catching, effective advertising.

We arrived at the lodge on Friday at five thirty and discovered that we'd beaten the remainder of the guests by a number of hours. That was nice, because it allowed Ron and me a chance to meet the owners and guides and interact with them on a far more personal level. By the time we finished our conversations over grilled hamburgers, we felt more like friends than guests, and it became abundantly clear to me that the managing owners, Doug and Jane Heidinger, were living exactly the life they wished to live. It was also apparent to us that they knew exactly how to work and manage their land to promote a large natural pheasant hatch and wild bird retention. Throughout the evening, I found myself gravitating to a corkboard on the wall in the main lodge to look at all the photos hanging there; the hunters decked out in blaze-orange vests and caps and iridescent roosters laid out on the ground, sparkling under the bright noonday sunshine.

The following morning, Ron and I were pleased to feel the Browning Belgium A5s swing and down numbers of pheasants that noisily burst from the corn and switchgrass. The old semi-autos, well-oiled and cared for, had spent too much time in the gun cabinet of late, and it was high time to run shells through them and dirty their bright bores again. Our group of fourteen hunters shot an astounding sixty-five roosters on Saturday and another forty-five during the few hours afield on Sunday morning. Any time you can honestly claim to shoot 110 roosters during the course of a day and a half of hunting is mighty impressive indeed. Considering the time we spent moving from field to field and a midday lunch break, the actual active hunting time worked out to about eight hours.

I'm not quite old enough to recall what others refer to as "yesteryear" hunting, or the good old days of pheasant hunting, but I can't imagine it was any better than what we experienced last weekend.

My father-in-law, Ron, and me after an unreal day of pheasant hunting at Dakota Wild Wings near Miller, South Dakota. I traded a write-up in a Midwest outdoor magazine for this hunt. It made for a nice piece, but I can't help but think that Ron and I definitely got the better half of this deal.

I plan to send off a colorful photo of our hunting party to the lodge, all of us looking deliriously happy standing and kneeling behind a mound of roosters at our feet. No doubt other skeptical hunters will see that picture tacked to the lodge's bragging board and wonder on a Friday evening, after they've finished supper and unpacked their clothing and gear, if their own hunting experience the next day will be as fantastic and memorable as ours. I have little doubt that it will be.

An Affordable Double

After purchasing a Browning BPS Upland Special 16-gauge last year, I thought that I was pretty well set. No need to look any further for a suitable upland bird-getter. No sir. I was all set to go. Then, at some point late last winter, I began to feel an itch for a classic double gun—a side-by-side—to complement the BPS and lend a bit of class to the gun safe. After all, a photo of a bird or two lying across the broken breech of a snazzy double gun is pretty tough to beat from an artistic standpoint.

Guns aren't getting any cheaper, and with two boys in the house who I hope will eagerly hunt with their dear old dad someday, I almost felt it my duty last month to pick up a nifty Huglu (pronounced *hoo-loo*) 20-gauge side-by-side with twenty-six-inch barrels, five chokes, and a single selective trigger. In addition to those requisite specifications, it was a pleasant surprise to find this reputable Turkish gunmaker willing to build their smaller gauge guns on matching frames offer hand-checkered Turkish walnut stocks and hand-engraved, case-hardened steel.

Simply put, the significance of a frame-to-gauge match means that my Huglu weighs in at just less than six pounds. Sticking 20-gauge barrels on a heavy 12-gauge frame would put my gun well within the seven-pound range. That is indeed an important consideration (and ultimately unacceptable) when you're carrying your shotgun in a muzzle-up position, stomping through heavy cover, and walking the woods for hours on end.

I should mention that the side-by-side I chose to purchase is one of a number of double guns out there on the market that are, in my opinion, very reasonably priced. By affordable, I mean between five hundred and one thousand dollars and a need on my part to sell some assorted stuff in order to offset the cost.

I found my particular gun online at a site called GunBroker. com. This gun auction site, like others out there on the internet, operates a lot like eBay. Sellers (usually brick-and-mortar shops located around the country) post their guns, along with accurate descriptions and photos, and buyers have the option to either place a bid or buy now. Buyers and sellers are rated, so finding a highly reputable dealer is as easy as looking at his or her numeric score. Of course, any gun that is purchased online must be shipped to a Federal Firearms License (FFL) dealer, and the buyer must complete all the necessary federal paperwork and pass all background checks.

There is, of course, an entire fraternity of side-by-side manufacturers out there offering guns with price tags that would momentarily stop your heart and make you wish you had a defibrillator close at hand. If you mention makers such as Grulla, AyA, and Arrieta to a modest hunter (I'm sorry, I couldn't help myself), you might fully expect to receive a look of incomprehension in return. After all, folks like you and me don't typically own and carry guns that cost fifty thousand dollars. Pay for a wing-shooting trip to Argentina for Córdoba doves and perdiz, and you'll definitely bump into a bunch of tweedy pipe-smokers who will know exactly what you're referring to. I can't speak for you, but I certainly don't breathe that type of rarified and aromatic air.

I did put that Huglu of mine through the paces this past weekend in northern Wisconsin, and I must say that I'm pleased as punch with its performance. It may sound weird to any of you nonhunters out there, but shooting this gun actually makes me smile. It is quick to the shoulder, and my eye finds the sight plane instantaneously. From a shot-to-kill ratio, my personal performance last weekend left something to be desired. But I have a brother-in-law who's willing to swear in a court of law that the birds we put up flushed well ahead and to the sides of our positions.

If you've always dreamed of owning and carrying an affordable side-by-side shotgun, now might be just the right time to make that purchase. There are plenty of reputable gunmakers out there offering double guns that won't break the bank yet provide quality workmanship and appointments you'd expect to see on guns costing thousands of dollars. In today's economy, it's important to buy smart and steer clear of quickly depreciating assets. Like my grandpa used to say, a good shotgun is always a good investment.

Brother-in-Law Stabs Self—Steals Headline from Governor Pawlenty

Thinking of worthwhile and interesting things to write about related to the great outdoors can sometimes be a real challenge. For instance, I once had an opportunity to attend the Governor's Big Buck Banquet, an annual event that kicks off the Governor's Deer Opener, but to be honest, there wasn't much to tell about that Friday evening that couldn't be read about in the Twin Cities' Sunday newspapers. The long and short of it was that once again the governor didn't have an opportunity to shoot a deer. In his defense, however, he did mention at the banquet that it's pretty tough to see deer—let alone shoot one—with choppers buzzing overhead and the woods teeming with Minnesota State Patrol security personnel.

On the other hand, the following day, I did witness my brother-in-law stab himself in the thigh with a big Buck Knife, which, you have to admit, is something you don't see every day and altogether too good to pass up from a writer's standpoint.

On opening morning, my brother-in-law, Mark, shot an impressive eight-point buck (the deer was trotting about sixty yards away, no less) with his new Mossberg 20-gauge, outfitted with a twenty-two-inch rifled barrel and 4X scope. Mark was full of "shucks" and "by gollys" when he talked about shooting that buck, but judging from where his single shot hit the deer, I doubt luck had too much to do with the final outcome.

Anyway, when it came time to eviscerate the beast, I played the typical supporting role, grabbing both front hooves while Mark positioned himself at the opposite end, starting with the breastbone and working his way down from there. The big Buck Knife must have gotten hung up on something around the deer's midsection, and Mark struggled a bit as he attempted to draw and sort of yank the blade toward himself. (Reads a bit like a Shakespeare tragedy, doesn't it?) The knife suddenly worked its way free and, quick as a wink, found Mark's inner thigh. I know what you're thinking, and I thought of it, too, the moment the blade tip snicked through Mark's heavy bib overalls and snazzy blue long johns: What about Mark's femoral artery? (That's the profunda femoris artery for you Latin fans out there.) Hooey, I mean, nick that baby and it's lights out in a big damn hurry, my friend.

Needless to say, I kept a keen eye on Mark for a minute or two following this incident. After I determined that he wasn't going to suddenly turn ghostly white and pitch over backward, I decided against quickly asking him for his gun collection, Toyota Tacoma pickup with the off-road package, and newly acquired eight-point rack.

Seriously though, when Mark's face registered concern a short time later and he mildly complained that his leg was beginning to stiffen up and smart, we inspected the site a bit closer and discovered a pretty good gash peeking out from behind the sliced fabric of his coveralls. At that point, I did give some serious thought to my recent refresher course in first aid and how to fashion a tourniquet with a belt.

I know Mark downplays this whole deal and will probably kill me for writing this, but he does have a few stitches in his leg as a reminder. When Mark asked the attending urgent care doctor in Stillwater about his injury and its proximity to that critical artery, the doctor replied, "Ach. You were a couple of inches away. Not even close."

You know, this mishap brings to mind some profound words of wisdom inscribed on a heavily lacquered cedar plaque. This plaque is a treasured family heirloom that proudly hangs in the in-laws' outdoor biffy at their cottage in northern Wisconsin. It occupies a prominent place on the wall right above the toilet tank, so being of the male persuasion, I'm naturally inclined to give it more of my undivided attention and deep consideration than the women and girls in the family. The plaque reads, "As you go through life, two rules will never bend: Never whittle toward yourself or pee against the wind."

I have to admit I went off on a bit of a tangent to work the toilet plaque into this article, but I think you know what I'm talking about, and aren't you thankful I did? I mean, jeesh, in light of this slightly exaggerated story, those truly are words to live by, aren't they?

THE GAME

He stood on the street corner in downtown Mercer, Wisconsin. It was hotter than Hades. His grandma—God rest her soul— liked to say on days like this that it was hotter than two hamsters farting in a wool sock.

He heard that Mercer was the place to find a gun with no questions asked. Stepping off the curb, he made his way across the empty street to the Wampum Shop. The word on the street was that the store's owner liked to make money, and he had trouble remembering customers—reassuring words to a guy looking for a gun on short notice.

Thankful to get out of the oppressive heat, he jerked the shop's old aluminum door open and stepped inside. The door banged closed, and he was instantly met by the overwhelming smell of cedar and cheap incense that walloped him like a prizefighter with a roll of nickels in his glove. The other thing worth noting was the big Indian standing near the entrance of the store. His arms were crossed, and he didn't look like he was in a very good mood. The Indian's eyes seemed to follow him all the way across the room to where the owner stood behind a counter.

"I need a piece and some ammo. I heard you're the man to talk to."

The man behind the counter looked down, sizing up his customer. "What sorta gun you lookin' for, stranger? I got all kinds. You got a big job to take care of? Maybe you need a big gun, eh?"

"No," the customer replied, shaking his head. "I need something small and light. Something I can keep in my pocket and not worry my pants will wind up around my ankles when I'm on the move." Looking in the glass case, he spotted just what he needed. "That one. I'll take that one, the pearl-handled revolver. And gimme a few boxes of ammo and throw in a pack of cigs while you're at it too. I'll take a box of Kings if you got 'em."

The stranger left the shop, happy to be done with his business, and maybe even happier to be out from under the watchful gaze of the big Indian, who hadn't so much as batted an eyelash the whole time he was talking to the shop owner. Ducking under an awning that offered some shade, the stranger hung a fresh King off his lower lip. He blew some chalky dust into the hot July air and thought about what he planned to do later in the day.

To keep his mind sharp on the ride back to the cabin, he silently played the alphabet game. He got hung up on the letter J. The letter J was always a tough one to spot. He opened the box of Kings and was somewhat surprised to see that he'd gone through nearly the whole pack. Once he started, it was tough to stop.

Later that evening his big brother, Anders, made him close his eyes and count to twenty while he dashed off around the corner of the cabin to hide. "Eighteen, nineteen, twenty . . . ready or not, here I come!" He checked one last time to make sure his new revolver was properly loaded as he cautiously began to stalk his opponent. He was good. He was only seven, but not too many could play the game any better.

A pair of tennis shoes betrayed Anders's position behind one of the parked vehicles in the driveway. He silently crept around the back of the pickup truck and squeezed off a bunch of shots: *Bang! Bang! Bang! Bang! Bang!* The new six-shooter, gleaming in the sunlight, flawlessly fed red paper caps up and out of the breach. Smoke hung lazily in the still air, and there was the sweet smell of gunpowder. It smelled like . . . victory. "I got you!" he yelled triumphantly. Anders never saw his little brother coming.

He had only one candy cigarette left in the box. He was saving it for this occasion. He shook out the last cavity stick, crunched it in half with his teeth, and then wiped a few smudges off the nickel finish of his new cap gun with the corner of his dirty T-shirt.

Augie didn't know when they'd get back to the Wampum Shop. Soon, he hoped. A Northwoods trading post was the only place a kid could get great stuff like cap guns, candy cigarettes, fake barf, and trick chewing gum that made your mouth turn black. Maybe Mom and Dad would take them tomorrow if the weather was too crummy to swim or fish. As usual, the store's wooden Indian would be there to greet them.

Fish Madness

Just the other day, I wondered why some anglers are compelled to behave far differently than other anglers. What possesses a small population of otherwise rational, clear-thinking men and women to defy reasonable conduct in their pursuit of fish?

In my mind, there are two distinct camps of anglers: fair-weather anglers that fish at convenient times, and stark raving lunatics (I proudly admit to being a card-carrying member of this particular group) that can read a nebulous report of fantastic fishing elsewhere and forgo everything else in life to get to these fish in a big hurry. If that weren't odd enough, we appear to do so with seemingly little to no thought of the time, inconvenience, or cost of getting there. What are the factors that compel some to drive untold distances to faraway places to target fish that may or may not cooperate once they've arrived?

I am one of many out there who suffer from a debilitating condition that I call Fish Madness. This condition has forced me to take day trips as far away as the Cascade River and other points along the North Shore of Lake Superior to chase steelhead, salmon, Kamloops trout, and lake trout. Before dawn, under a starlit sky and clearly closer to sleeping than wakefulness, I've loaded my vehicle full of fishing equipment and hit the road with only a cup of strong coffee, a roadmap, and blind hope to guide me.

Some years ago an old buddy, Paul Bury, and I raised a particular muskie a number of times over a sunken island on Leech Lake. The big fish would follow our bucktail spinners and jerk baits right to the boat, only to slowly sink from view, as if our eyes had played a trick on us and he hadn't been there at all. The following weekend, I ran up there alone on a crisp fall day to see if I could finally fool that fish. After only a couple of casts over the underwater hump with an oversize, deep-diving crank bait, there he was again. A shadowy, menacing form that suddenly materialized from the cobalt-blue depths. He followed that plug to the side of the boat, where I quickly began to perform a figure eight with only a scant couple feet of line off the end of my rod. I ripped the bait sideways. It hadn't made it beyond the first loop in the water when the big muskie opened its gaping maw, flicked his powerful tail, and inhaled it. I never once regretted spending seven hours in the car for that solitary, knee-knocking experience.

The other day I took a peek at a fly-fishing site on the internet to see how some friends had recently fared on our Minnesota and Wisconsin streams and rivers. Mike Wemlinger, from Hudson, Wisconsin, posted a story and stunning pictures that exemplify why some die-hard anglers buck conventional wisdom while at the same time manage to only deepen the mystery, failing—thankfully—to unravel it.

Mike wrote,

> You ever have one of those nights when you just can't get to sleep? Last night I had one of those nights and I lay there and tossed and turned. While I was thrashing about, I got to thinking, *Why not just get up and take a quick trip to the Brule River? Heck, it's only about two and a half hours if I push it.* So I finally got out of bed at four, made a pot of coffee and took a shower. I checked the weather and found that it would be a cold, windy and, best of all, rainy day. I filled the thermos and hit the road.

Does that sound like the thoughts and actions of a rational man? Well, most would argue no. Those who would question this line of thinking are the folks who fish at times when the weather is nice and the time is convenient. You see, Mike also suffers from Fish Madness, a malady for which there is no cure. He drove a number of hours to catch a single magnificent fish, a wild and powerful steelhead capable of straightening hooks and reducing grown men and women to tears.

Life is pretty short. Sure, warm beds are nice and comfortable, but some of us are compelled to put ourselves through some hardship and inconvenience to experience magical moments—fleeting opportunities that come around only once. In this case, Mike would've denied himself a rare moment on the famed Brule River, engaged in hand-to-fin combat with a big fish in a hard current without a soul in sight.

If science and pharmaceutical companies ever developed a cure for this madness, I really have my doubts doctors would write too many prescriptions. What, a drug that prevents us from making last-minute, half-baked plans to experience some of the best things life has to offer? Now that sounds like a whole different sort of madness to me, and I'll have no part of it.

A good Grouse Hunt

i invited my eight-year-old son, Anders, to walk the woods with me in search of grouse for the first time last weekend. Judging by his apparent excitement and the utterance of a single word—"Whoa!"—following an explosive flush and the bark of my Browning 16-gauge, I can only assume that his first grouse hunt was quite a revelation.

The birds—six in total, four shots taken, and zero hits—were skittish on that wet, breezy day. Evasive measures included skulking some distance ahead of us through the undergrowth before taking to the air amid the dense stands of young aspens.

As we quietly walked over the sodden leaves littering the trail that would eventually lead us back to the vehicle, I began to hear a faint clicking noise that I found unnerving. When I stopped walking, the clicking stopped, so I carefully took the time to check my vest pockets for the source and mumbled, "Where is that noise coming from?" It was then that I looked backward to discover Anders wearing four empty shotshells on the fingers of his left hand. Sensing my confusion and slight annoyance, Anders looked up at me with a big toothy grin and wiggled his fingers, causing the brass ends of the shells to click together. We had a pretty good laugh over that. I did, however, make him give up the empty shells for the remainder of our walk.

When we arrived back at the cottage, I was feeling a bit down at having missed four birds with my new Browning, despite the fact that they were low percentage shots. It was Anders's sunny disposition that immediately brightened my mood when he reported to all who awaited us: "Dad almost shot four grouse!" I realized then that Anders would make an outstanding hunting partner in the years to come.

As I had hoped would happen, the following two days afforded me just as many high percentage shots, and the Browning did indeed swing true and find its mark. Two birds were admired and photographed in hand before being slipped into the game bag.

I recall Anders's hunting report and the excitement he must have felt as we walked the woods together. I realize now more than ever that it's rewarding enough to simply be out there enjoying the splendor of fall, and that there is no such thing as a bad grouse hunt.

Hat For Sale

I f you were to ask my wife about the various neuroses that plague me, she would readily place my thing for hats up near the top of the list.

I believe hats are essentially utilitarian, and there is a particular hat for every season and every reason. Of course, with our four seasons here in Minnesota and the countless outdoor activities to choose from in each of those seasons, well, you get the picture. A guy like me can wind up with a lot of hats.

There is, however, one hat I cherish above all others, and that is my trusty Filson Tin Cloth Packer Hat. What led me to write about this hat is the fact that I recently discovered I must sell it. The reason for (and terms of) the sale can be found below, in an excerpt from the actual ad I ran on eBay.

Up for sale is my beloved Filson Tin Cloth Packer Hat. It's about fifteen years old and, as you can plainly see by the photos, perfectly broken in and seasoned to perfection. I'd estimate that there's a good forty years of life left in it. You could buy a new Filson hat for about $50, but it'd take you at least a decade to get your new hat looking as cool as my hat. And isn't looking good what it's all about?

So why am I selling it? Well, I grabbed the Filson the other day to go fish a heavy caddis hatch on the famed Kinnickinnic River when I discovered that the hat no longer fits my head. I did recently suffer from a bout of high-altitude cerebral edema

I wasn't sure how I could possibly provide a caption for a hat, but I do vividly recall that my wife, Su, was not too pleased to learn how much I paid for this Filson hat. I asked her, If you pay more money for a really good hat and it lasts a lifetime, how much are you really spending over the life of the hat? Su didn't buy that cockamamie logic, and I don't blame her.

caused from skiing too high in the Colorado Rockies. Did my swollen brain make my head bigger? Is that possible? I don't know, I'm not a doctor. All I know is my favorite hat won't fit my bean and it upsets me to no end.

You should know that the fishing mojo in this hat is excellent, and its provenance is beyond reproach. Over the years, this hat and I have spent some serious quality time on the water. We've fished some good hatches together, and this old hat has seen innumerable trout brought to hand, from brookies in northern Wisconsin and Maine to Colorado cutthroat, Montana browns and Arkansas rainbows.

In addition, this hat has been a trusted companion on wild steelhead and salmon rivers on Lake Superior tributaries, from the Devil Track River north of Grand Marais to the Brule River along the south shore.

So just how groovy is this hat? This Filson is the sort of hat you'd dip in a cool stream and allow your steed to drink from, all the while stroking his mane and saying soothing, cowboy-like stuff such as, "Thar ya go, ol' boy. Drink up now, y'hear? The trail's long 'n' water's scarce in these here parts." Can you see it? Well I sure can, and I look good too. Although, with the eight brass grommets on the sides of the hat for ventilation, the horse would have to drink quickly before all the water drained out onto the ground and your cowboy boots.

I digress. Back to the hat.

The hat really must go to a deserving person. If you're a fly angler, you might be the right person to wear this hat. But that might not be enough. Folks will expect that you know your stuff, like the proper Latin names for most of the major aquatic invertebrates. You won't be able to BS your way through a good *Ephemerella subvaria* hatch wearing the Filson. Telling a fellow angler, "Well, them little bugs were, oh, yea high and so long," using your thumb and forefinger as a gauge, simply won't cut it.

Oh, and if you're a spin fisherman with a penchant for throwing big silver and gold spinners loaded with treble hooks, don't even entertain the thought of bidding on this hat. I have the sneaking suspicion some of you out there are night crawler and bobber anglers. Maybe one of those ball caps with the curly straws that hold beer cans might be more your style. No Filson for you!

So, do you have what it takes to wear the Filson? Squeamish about plopping a used, fifteen-year-old hat on your head? If you were like me, you wouldn't give it a second thought. Heck, if you were like me, you'd wear the hat after your horse drank from it—slobber and all. We're those kind of men. Real men. Fly fishers. Trout chasers. Filson men. Somebody cue up the studly cowboy music, pan out and . . . cut. That's a wrap.

great winter memories are made at outdoor ice rinks

In the neighborhood where I grew up, there was no such thing as "ice time." I grew up on the mean rinks of Golden Valley, a first-ring suburb of Minneapolis. I'm not talking about the old money neighborhoods in and around Tyrol Hills that tickle Benilde-St. Margaret's and the Lincoln Del off Highway 100. No sir. I'm talking about the northwest corner of Golden Valley, just south of New Hope—also known at the time as "No Hope," where dreams of making it big died young and everything looked gray. Think of a monochromatic Pennsylvania steel town, add an extra dash of bleakness and desperation, and you have my neighborhood.

As I said, "ice time" was a very foreign term to us. It conjured up images of cavernous arenas and sports domes with perfect sheets of ice, complete with Zambonis, referees, penalty boxes, and scoreboards. No, where I'm from, ice time meant some pimply-faced goon hot-boxing a heater behind the warming house was going to slam your face against the ice if you cracked wise. After that, depending on whether or not you had any buddies around, you'd all drop your wool-lined leather choppers and all hell would break loose. Thank goodness our dads made us write our initials on the backs of our choppers in big block letters so we could sort them out following these melees.

As a kid I remember spending entire weekends at the rink, which was a half block from our house. On weekdays, my brother and I would lace up our skates in the house right after school and walk the short distance to the rink on our rubber blade guards. When Mom would yell for us out the kitchen window at five o'clock, we'd run home for dinner, scarf down our meal, and get back to the rink and skate until seven o'clock or so. Our ice time was free and there was no shortage of it. I sometimes wonder if kids today are getting enough of that same ice time on our area rinks. My boys and I surely don't see throngs of skaters at our local rink here in Taylors Falls. Of course, it has been quite cold lately. Perhaps numbers will increase once this Siberian air leaves us.

I'm still a huge fan of public ice rinks. I believe wholeheartedly that the best skating can be had on our public rinks. Some of my very best memories as a kid include pickup hockey games down at the neighborhood rink. In other words, there's a lot to be said about unscheduled outdoor ice time. The best thing about a public rink is you can skate whenever you want.

It is encouraging to know that if city park and recreation dollars are hard to come by in these tough economic times, you certainly wouldn't know it from looking at our local rinks. There is an unsung group of private individuals and fire departments working all winter long to keep our rinks in outstanding shape. I recently heard from a reliable source that donated hockey boards might find their way to the rink in our town of Taylors Falls. I'm hoping that's true.

One evening last week, before my boys and I hit the warming house to take off our skates and get home in time for dinner, I decided to uncork a slap shot. You know, see if the Old Man could still bring it. I judged my distance to be somewhere between the blue line and red line. A moment after whiffing the puck and before thudding against the ice, I recall my body contorting in midair. Anders and Augie, who are quite good on their skis and capable of performing all sorts of ski tricks in the terrain park at Wild Mountain, claim that I performed an off-axis-tail-grab 540. I just remember being splayed out on the ice, staring up at all the pretty stars in the night sky while my boys simultaneously shouted, "Sweeeeeeet!"

Needless to say, I refused to allow the night to end on that note, so I pried myself off the ice with as much dignity as I could muster and circled around again for a second try. This time, I made sure to keep my head down. My Mikko Koivu–like slapper left the ice at a blistering speed and rose menacingly as it neared the net. If a goalie were standing there in the crease, I seriously doubt he could've gotten his glove up fast enough to cover the three hole. "Tink!" The puck ricocheted off the cross pipe and sailed into the woods, lost until the spring melt.

Yes, more good memories of skating with my boys on a public rink. I highly recommend grabbing your skates and visiting your local rink. Outdoor skating is one of the best ways to enjoy our Minnesota winters.

Healthy Eating is Not for the Faint of Heart

I'm trying to eat better. Lord knows I am. It's just that some foods seem to routinely sidetrack my lackadaisical efforts. Eating only the right foods day in and day out is tough, particularly with the advent of the dollar menu and those little cheese-filled crackers you find in gas stations.

You should first understand that my wife, Su, is the healthiest person I know, so the pressure is on at the home front. She faithfully gets up before the sun every morning, throws on her stretchy clothes, and does some really far-out bendy things to a public television show. I think the show is called *How to Be Thin and Taut and Look Better Than Your Lumpy, Hail-Damaged Husband*, or something along those lines.

The other morning, I came downstairs and nearly had a heart attack. It looked as though a semi truck had repeatedly run over my dear Su in our own living room. She was upside down on the floor and appeared to have suffered a number of compound fractures, her limbs pointing this way and that. About the time I made a lunge for the phone to dial 911, she waggled her right foot in the air, smiled, and said, "Good morning." Aha. Yoga. The scorpion pose, to be precise. Look it up. My spine would snap like dried kindling if I even thought of trying it. When I realized she was OK, I headed to the kitchen to brew coffee and look for a chocolate chip cookie.

For a few years we were members of an organic dairy and vegetable farm cooperative located in Wisconsin. It seemed to me that we paid a lot of money to essentially roll the dice with the locusts and hail and other biblical plagues that might work to create a zero return on our investment. I also recall reading a blurb on the side of a glass milk bottle explaining that the milk in the bottle was sloshing around inside a cow the very morning it was delivered to our doorstep. I don't think I've had a glass of milk since.

I could identify most of the veggies the farm delivered each week, but every once in a while we'd wind up with stuff in our fridge that was a real head-scratcher. It was only after I spent a fair amount of time on Google searching "obscure vegetables" that I realized there's a lot of stuff out there I'm not willing to eat. I'm not exactly sure, but kale might be one of them.

Even though we currently don't belong to a farm cooperative, unidentifiable veggies still find their way into our crisper. Just this morning I tested Su by picking up a bumpy yellow thing that looked like a miniature UFO. "What's this thing?" I asked. "I'm not sure," Su replied. "Some sort of squash I think." Now I'm really confused. She does the grocery shopping and she doesn't know what she bought? Maybe it just looked too healthy to pass up.

For a couple of weeks last year there was a head of something in our fridge that brought to mind a really creepy scene from the movie *Invasion of the Body Snatchers*. I'm not kidding. I would close the fridge door and go to bed feeling 100 percent certain something really insidious and scary was going to ooze up the stairs and take me in the middle of the night.

Last Friday I had a guiding job for trout on the Whitewater River near Elba, Minnesota. Up until that date, I thought I'd been doing pretty well as far as my diet was concerned. I even opted for the soup and salad bar when my fishing clients and I broke for lunch on Friday at the Elba Tower House restaurant.

Driving home north along Highway 61 on Saturday, I was thinking about the good food choices I was making and feeling pretty good about myself. Then it hit me. The first strong hunger pangs of the day socked me in the guts just as I approached Lake City. As I was halfway through town, my hand instinctively left the wheel and snapped on the left turn signal. No! I'm powerless! Don't undo the health benefits of the salad bar! It was futile thinking on my part, of course. My Isuzu Trooper, like the Millennium Falcon in *Return of the Jedi*, was being pulled along helplessly by a fast-food Death Star tractor beam.

In less than twelve parsecs (that's the same amount of time the Millennium Falcon needed to make the Kessel Run, by the way), I found myself speaking to a less-than-enthusiastic teenager through a drive-through speaker. "Like, welcome to Trans Fattie's. Can I take your order?" I felt enormously guilty as I briefly glanced at the salad choices before ordering. "I'll take two double cheeseburgers and a fry off the dollar menu. Oh, and a medium Diet Coke." A lot of help that Diet Coke would do.

Well, Rome wasn't built in a day. Like I said, I'm trying to eat better, but every once in a while I get sidetracked. If kale and string beans tasted like a double cheeseburger, I'd be the healthiest guy in the world.

SOME THOUGHTS ARE BEST KEPT TO MYSELF

This is tough to admit, but this summer, as I faithfully attend my son's baseball games, it has taken all my strength to avoid becoming mentally unglued and morphing into one of those ranting, spittle-spewing Sports Dads that are universally reviled.

I think it's safe to say that we'd just as soon not know these dads on a personal level. I mean, if they get that worked up over a baseball or soccer game played by third- and fourth-grade children, would they behave the same way in other areas of their lives? Or worse?

I'm happy to report that I haven't crossed that line. So far, I've managed to keep negative comments to myself and have yet to say anything out loud that would irrevocably cause shame and embarrassment to me or my son.

But what if my mind tricks me one day and I do in fact verbalize what I'm thinking? What if my brain momentarily lapses and my keep-it-to-yourself words and my out-loud words get mixed up? Oh boy, I hope that day never arrives. "Hey kid, pick up the ball with your bare hand! When the ball is dead on the ground, pick it up with your bare hand, not your glove! See that big leather thing on your left hand? Don't use it to pick up the ball. Could somebody just kill me now? Please, that'd be great. Thanks so much."

You get the picture. I've said stuff like that over and over in my mind, but I wouldn't dare say it out loud, particularly when the

For the love of God and everything good in this world, pick up a baseball with your bare hand when it's just sitting there in the tall grass. In youth baseball, this move has turned countless singles into inside-the-park home runs.

———————————

kid flubbing a play isn't my kid. By the way, if there are any baseball or softball dads or moms out there reading this who deny feeling what I feel, well, I'm sorry, but I simply don't believe you. At the games you might appear to be virtuous and cool as a cucumber on the outside, but inside you're just as nuts as I am. Who are you trying to kid? Save that righteousness for Sunday. Today is Tuesday and on Tuesday we play baseball.

The following is an actual keep-it-to-yourself rant that almost leaked out of my mouth one night at a game after the batter absolutely scalded the ball into the gap between third and short. Thankfully I stopped it in time. "Uh-oh, where's the left fielder? Oh, for the love of God and everything that is good in this world, get the ball! Don't try to dig the ball out of the tall grass with your glove! Aaargh! What have I been trying to telepathically teach you kids for the past month about picking up baseballs that are just lying there on the ground? Hit the cutoff! Where's the shortstop? Short, you're the relay man! Oh no, the runner just rounded third. It's another base-emptying single. What's the score now, twenty-seven to four? My left arm is starting to go numb. Does anybody have a small paper sack I can breathe into? Medic!"

There is something that keeps my lunatic rants locked safely inside my head and prevents me (so far anyway) from spewing them out loud, and that is the fact that my boy is only ten years old. Every once in a while it's a good idea to remind ourselves that our kids are in fact just that—kids. Our kids are out there to please us and have fun and learn a thing or two along the way. Young psyches are pretty fragile, so we'd better handle them with care.

Why is it that some parents get so emotionally caught up in youth league sports? My reasoning is that we're simply wired that way and there's no point in denying it. It's human nature, and human nature is hard to overcome, but it's certainly not impossible. The trick is to demonstrate to yourself and others (but most importantly, to your kid) that you're calm and supportive and not a raving basket case. Sometimes it's tough, there's no doubt about it. I want my boy to succeed and play as well as he can possibly play, but at the same time, I am tempering those feelings with real-world expectations and unfailing support. If my kid flubs a play, I sure wouldn't want some other parent to verbally tee off on him. If that happened, there's a good chance I'd wind up on the TV show *America's Most Wanted*. I can hear the host, John Walsh, now: "If you see this man, do not approach him or talk to him about baseball. Call the authorities right away. The suspect is an out-of-shape forty-nine-year-old male with a slight limp due to a bad hammy and pinched sciatic nerve . . ."

OK, back to the game. It's the bottom of the sixth inning and our team might actually pull out a win tonight. What did I just see? Oh lordy. Tell me I didn't see what I just saw! He was safe! He was safe! "Hey Ump, what game are you watching? The runner beat the throw by a mile! What's that? Oh, I see. Well, you should've told us you live in an upside-down backward world and call games using an entirely different set of baseball rules. In that case, great call, you're a genius!"

See what I mean? Thank goodness most of us are able to keep our comments to ourselves. If you're one of those parents who can't, well, try to go easy on my kid. Like all the kids out there, he's doing the best he can.

i'm willing to share the coveted fish fry crown

i feel sorry for people who say they don't like to eat fish. Living in this part of the country, you wouldn't think that there'd be too many folks among us who proclaim that they hate fish. It's really not their fault. We shouldn't look down on those who don't eat fish. They are victims. Yes, at some unfortunate time in their lives, they fell victim to fish fillet abuse. Just like there are countless people who routinely render a perfectly good cut of venison unfit for human consumption, there are at least an equal number of people who consistently clean their fish improperly, store it incorrectly, and have the nerve (the nerve!) to prepare and serve crummy-tasting fish.

Let's get something perfectly straight. I don't like it when somebody announces to the world that they are the best at something or another. "I'm the best fisherman." "I'm the best hunter." "I know everything, blah, blah, blah . . ." Yeah, whatever, here's your trophy, now hit the trail, Jessup. That's why writing this makes me a bit uncomfortable. You see, I am the best at something or another, and it has taken me a number of years to admit it publicly, but I think it's time I get it off my chest.

I am, without a shadow of a doubt, the best shore lunch fish fryer in the world. Well, actually, in the entire universe. If they held a Mr. Universe fish fry competition, they'd slap a big shiny frying pan crown on my head and I'd wind up wearing one of those ribbon sashes over my shoulder and walking down a runway, waving to the crowd with that funny pageant wave that looks like you're rubbing wax off the hood of a car. I used to hit Otter Tail Lake for the walleye opener, and I'll readily admit that there are a few buddies up near Perham, Minnesota, who produce fried fish that gives my own a run for the money, but I doubt those boys will run out and buy this book, so they don't count. So there. This is my book and I can play any way I want to, fair or unfair.

As I mentioned, it has taken a number of years to fine-tune and perfect my shore lunch fish fry. The actual frying of the fillets is, arguably, the easy part. It's how the fillets are cleaned, stored, prepped, and everything else you do prior to frying the fish that really counts. Don't laugh, but I've had people sample my fish—folks who told me previously that they flat out didn't like fish—suddenly drop to their knees, throw their hands in the air, and proclaim themselves to be saved. (It's tough, but I do refrain from placing my hand on their foreheads and shoving them to the ground like a Southern preacher.) Other times, folks who taste my fish will get all teary-eyed and stare at me. Very unnerving. That's the moment I drop the slotted spatula and run, because I know these people will chase me around the backyard, tackle me, and attempt to hug me. I don't like being tackled, and my wife gets nervous about the hugging part. It's time other fish fryers out there share the love. But most of all, I feel so bad for all of the hapless and miserable fish haters out there that I'm willing to unveil my most private secrets. Sharpen those number two pencils, because I'm going to lay it on you right now.

At the fillet board, have a container of ice water at the ready. After each fillet is removed from the fish, just toss those babies into the water. Don't worry about final cleaning yet. Next, rinse the fillets (one at a time) under cold running water. Rub the fillets between your hands like you would a bar of soap. The fillet is perfectly clean when you feel friction between the fillet and your hands. If you can snap your fingers after cleaning a fillet without flinging a gob of translucent fish snot across the kitchen, you've done it right.

Next, soak the fillets in a container of buttermilk for an hour or so prior to frying. I know buttermilk smells sour, but trust me. While the fillets soak, keep them *out* of the refrigerator. Refrigeration is a cardinal sin. Fish should always be near room temperature prior to frying. If you fry cold fillets, the oil will rapidly cool when you add the cold fish, resulting in rubbery fish with a soggy coating. Rubbery fish is bad, and people will not drop to their knees or hug you if you serve them wet, rubbery fish fillets.

After the soaking, remove the fillets from the buttermilk and place them in a colander in the sink; when they are shaken in the dry Shore Lunch coating mix, the fillets should be moist, but not dripping wet. Dripping wet fillets will cause the mixture to get gooey and sticky.

Preheat your vegetable oil. I use a propane cooker and a large pot for frying, but the stove top works perfectly well, too, provided that it's capable of achieving and maintaining oil at 375 degrees. You will be deep-frying, so the oil should be three to four inches deep. Here's a bit of a secret: it's not easy to "eyeball" the temperature of oil. In other words, without the aid of a thermometer, you'll never know if the oil is at 325, 350, or 375 degrees. To achieve a crisp outer coating in a short amount of time, fish must be fried at or near 375 degrees, so if you don't have a large candy/deep-fry thermometer that clips to the side of the pot, run out and get one.

While the oil is preheating, combine one or two tablespoons Cajun spice seasoning and about one cup of dry packaged Shore Lunch in a heavy plastic bag. My favorite Shore Lunch comes in a black box. You know the one.

When the oil is to temperature, add four to six fillets to the bag with the Shore Lunch mixture. Add some air to the bag and twist the top closed before shaking. The air allows the fillets to separate and prevents them from sticking together.

Carefully lower the coated fillets into the oil and gently move them around a bit. The fillets should take no more than about two minutes to firm up and achieve that medium-brown color. Once the fillets are firm, remove them from the oil and place them concave side down onto paper towels and immediately sprinkle each fillet lightly with lemon pepper seasoning.

I need to mention a few additional things that are terribly important. If you plan to freeze your fillets to thaw and eat at a later date, do not freeze the fillets in water. At some point, we've all seen our dear old granny open the freezer and whip out the block of bluegill fillets that were stored in stinky, yellow water inside a cardboard milk container. You may as well throw out that fish. Instead, take a meal's worth of moist fillets and tightly wrap them in plastic wrap, as you would wrap a piece of meat in butcher paper: roll, fold the ends across the top, and roll again. You can roll up a number of packages and place them in one large zippered freezer bag. Press the air out of the bag before zipping it completely closed. When you want one meal of fish, unzip the bag and take out one plastic-wrapped serving of fillets. Fish stored in this manner will taste fresh for months and months down the line. Pretty slick, eh?

So that's about all there is to it. Easy really. I've decided that it's lonely at the top and it's high time I shared the coveted Frying Pan Crown with others. With every good fish fry, together we can save and convert the souls of many of the lost and confused fish haters out there.

Bon appétit.

i cast and i cast, but i don't catch any fish

i experienced some stressful circumstances leading up to the date that I took my Certified Casting Instructor exams through the Federation of Fly Fishers. It began when the federation informed me I could take my exams on October 10 in Richland Center, Wisconsin. That's a little less than four hours each way, which isn't too bad a drive. My plan was to get on the road really early that morning, take the tests, and drive back the same day.

Well, not long after that, I received another email explaining that the Richland Center exam opportunity evaporated, and that if I wished to take the exams, I'd need to do it a week earlier at the Federation of Fly Fishers Southern Council Conclave, held on October 3 in Mountain Home, Arkansas. Oh, and I had to commit to a decision within a week. (Since the other available testing sites are located in Malmköping, Sweden; Schimmert, Netherlands; and Moscow, Russia, I figured a twenty-six-hour round trip drive didn't sound too bad after all.)

So you can imagine what I was doing a lot of leading up to my trip to Arkansas. You got it. Casting, casting, casting. I practiced on either my neighbor's back lawn or the field at Taylors Falls Elementary School. Armed with my rod and reel, a hundred-foot measuring tape, and orange safety cones, I set up my mock testing area and cast.

My routine was to run through each of the required casts and analyze loop shapes, changes in the casting arc, power application, and stroke length, to name a few. The only effective way to practice the instructional portion of the exam (when candidates are asked to explain and demonstrate a wide range of casts and the theory behind these casts) was to talk out loud to myself as I ran through each question on the test. In other words, I would talk to people who weren't really there. Seriously, if somebody had offered me the choice between practicing fly casting for two hours every day and getting smacked repeatedly in the head with a ball-peen hammer, I think I'd choose the hammer. The flat side, please. Thank you very much.

I recall a particular evening standing in the St. Croix River and practicing my roll cast as the sun was setting and a light drizzle began to fall. In that moment, it occurred to me how silly all this casting stuff might appear to the outside world. I was wearing shorts and knee-high rubber boots and looking rather goofy when I noticed an older gentleman fishing off the public pier just upstream of my position. This is how our brief conversation unfolded:

"Ya catchin' any?" the old guy asked.

"I'm not fishing," I replied.

The old angler, puzzled, cautiously continued. "Sure looks like you're fishing to me."

"I'm practicing my roll cast. I need to cast fifty feet and the fly has to land within eighteen inches of a floating target." It was then that I began to really hear myself talk and I started to get a little concerned.

The old guy chuckled a bit nervously and added, "Maybe the fish don't know you're practicing and one of them will bite your fly."

"Won't do much good," I replied softly, hoping I wouldn't be heard. "There's no hook. I'm using a yarn fly."

I surmised something rather simple from that odd exchange: in this life, you're either a fly-casting geek studying the minutiae of an off-shoulder roll cast (and in turn making life and the pursuit of happiness far more complicated and elusive than it needs to be), or you're a guy sipping Old Style beer from a can while staring at a big orange plastic bobber. I can guarantee you that one of us on that river that evening didn't appear to have both oars in the water, and that guy was me. After all, which one of us appeared to be fishing in the dark and rain without a hook?

You've all probably heard Einstein's definition of insanity: "Insanity is doing the same thing over and over again and expecting different results." To the outside world, the sight of a guy intently scrutinizing fly line as it travels through the air must seem strange, particularly when it appears as if each cast is identical. But I can assure you that each cast is indeed different, and slight adjustments in the arc, line speed, or path of the rod tip will produce vastly different results.

Those facts are of little consolation, though. I've come to realize that attempts to explain what I'm doing to curious onlookers does me no good, and I indeed must appear to others as I truly am: a guy who mutters to himself while casting a fly rod with no hook on the end of his line.

Minnesota Bound
Pays Another Visit

I internalize stress. Talking to me, you might get a sense that nothing bothers me, but it does. With me, elevated stress manifests itself in two ways: too much gas and too little sleep. It'd be pretty tough to dedicate an entire column to my unearthly gas troubles, so I'll share with you my recent tale of sleepless nights brought on by high anxiety.

Recently, I experienced nearly two full weeks of fitful, restless sleep that had me up at all hours of the night. It got to the point where I seriously considered paying a visit to my doctor. I suspected a week or so into it that something was nagging at me, but I just couldn't put my finger on the source.

Well, beginning last Saturday night, I began to once again sleep like a log, and wouldn't you know it, it was the night following a day-long taping of *Minnesota Bound* up at Seven Pines Lodge, where I teach fly casting and guide lodge guests for stream trout.

Andy Warhol once predicted that everybody would be famous for fifteen minutes. I thought I'd cashed in my allotted time back in 2003, when we taped our first *Minnesota Bound* segment at Seven Pines. Well, Ron and the rest of the staff at Ron Schara Productions thought things went so well the first time around, they decided to pay another visit to the lodge last weekend. So I guess I got lucky and was generously granted a half hour of fleeting fame. Not too shabby for a homely mutt like me, I guess.

This upcoming segment will feature Schara's director of operations, Kelly Jo McDonnell, and her father, Jim, on the stream with yours truly. They were new to the sport, so I ran them through a complete session of casting instruction, where they did remarkably well and picked up the basics very quickly. From there, we all hit Knapp Creek, where they would apply their newly acquired skills and, I hoped, fool a few resident trout.

There are a lot of things that can (and often do) occur that are beyond my control when I'm on the stream with clients. It's not uncommon to see otherwise calm, cool, and collected casting pupils become stark raving lunatics when they hook their first trout. Or sometimes the trout inexplicably fall victim to a stream-wide lockjaw pandemic and refuse to open their mouths. I always get a bad case of flop sweat when that happens.

Now I had Steve Plummer, Schara's three-time Emmy Award–winning director of videography, behind his enormous camera sitting on a tripod, waiting for something exciting to happen. Exciting as in catching a trout. Jeepers, talk about stress. Fishing isn't supposed to be stressful, but it sure felt that way to me last Saturday, waiting for either Kelly or Jim to catch the first fish of the day.

I already told you that my sleeping patterns snapped back into alignment last weekend, so you probably figured out that everything went well with the shoot. I'm happy to report that the day I spent with the Schara folks couldn't have gone better. Kelly and her dad caught numerous trout, and their enthusiasm for the outdoors and each other was highly infectious. If you catch the segment and get a sense that we all got along famously and had a great time, it's because that's the way it really happened.

During the past four years, I've made some good friends at Schara Productions. I haven't met a single person from their outfit who wasn't friendly and a lot of fun to be around. They produce a distinctive outdoor program that focuses not merely on fish and game, but on unique human-interest stories that relate to the outdoors. This segment will showcase a really neat father and daughter relationship, and I feel very fortunate to have played a part in creating the show. I lost some sleep worrying about the outcome of that day's video shoot, but it was well worth it.

i never miss

If I'd been alive back in the Old West, I'm pretty sure folks would've hired me to shoot stuff. I never thought of myself as being anything so disagreeable and unsavory as a bounty hunter scouring the plains for outlaws. No, for some reason, I always had dangerous critters in mind. Sort of a traveling pest control business, but on a much grander scale.

I see myself clip-clopping down a dusty main street as men push through creaky saloon doors, their shifty eyes peering at me under a bright noonday sun. I also see a distraught woman running alongside my steed as I make my way to the sheriff's office, pleading, "Bad Brown, there's a big, mean grizzly bear terrorizin' our town! Our children ain't safe! Can ya git him?" I'd pull back on the reins and tip my white Stetson back on my forehead. After carefully working the wad of sunflower seeds packed in my cheek, I'd spit out an empty hull and reply, "Yes ma'am. Here's my business card. If you'll kindly look on the back there, it plainly reads that I ain't never missed." The front of the card, of course, would show a picture of me squinting dead-eyed down the barrel of my trusty 12-gauge, just like those famous old shots of Annie Oakley on the posters for Buffalo Bill's Wild West show.

Yes, for many years that was my daydream. My overactive imagination got plenty of miles out of that fantasy too. Because when it comes to shooting—particularly at deer—I never miss.

That is, until last Saturday, when the unthinkable happened.

Late that morning, I took careful aim on a good buck standing broadside about twenty-five yards from my stand. I lined up the fiber optic sights, slowly squeezed off a round, then watched in puzzled disbelief as a half year's worth of perfectly good venison bounded unscathed into the thick undergrowth. What made it doubly unbearable was the manner in which the deer fled. He bounced away stiff-legged, just like the *Looney Tunes* anthropomorphic French skunk, Pepé Le Pew. I suppose it could've been the wind, but I swear I heard him mumble just before disappearing into a thicket, "You meesed, mon ami! How fortunate for me. Perhaps your luck will be better next time, no?" Well, it was either the wind or I seriously need to dial back on my cartoon viewing.

Anyway, last Saturday I joined the lowly ranks of the Mortal Hunters Club. I am now officially listed in the 2012 edition of *Who's Who in Hunting* as "Mr. Whiff." I was even told that if you look up Barney Fife, under his picture are the words, "See also Dan Brown."

My family is running out of meat in the freezer, and I'm running out of time on the calendar. I'd better sharpen up and get a deer. No more fooling around. I'll allow one more encounter with a deer to shoot straight and redeem myself. If I whiff again, I guess I'll have to change the backside of those cards of mine to read, "I ain't never missed . . . well, almost never." It just doesn't have the same ring to it, does it?

OLD EarL HaD iT PreTTy gOOD

One evening, as I lay in bed patiently waiting for my two-year-old to fall asleep after reading books, a smile crept over my face. I was remembering a cool fall day, ten or so years before, when an old-timer, Earl Snell of Manitowish Waters, Wisconsin, reluctantly sold his prized fishing boat to my father-in-law, Ron.

I remember that at some point in our conversation, I was leaning up against the old Starcraft when Earl, who spent most of the day with a sizable wad of chewing tobacco in his cheek (as evidenced by the strategically placed Folgers cans in the boat and near the back door of his house), spit a brown gob of snoose on my SOREL boot and said in a wavering voice, "Goddamn it, I hate to have to sell her, but I guess I'm gettin' too old to fish . . . Damn it, annaway."

Earl, who was an old fishing buddy of Ron's dad, was ninety-something at the time. Unfortunately for Earl, it simply got to the point where he had become a growing concern and real liability on their fishing trips. His physical state of disrepair had progressed to the point where getting him in and out of vehicles and boats began to burn up the better part of the day.

Clearly, he was too old to do a lot of things, including seeing exactly where he was spitting. But, in talking with him, it was abundantly clear that of all the things in life that he missed, he'd miss fishing in his old boat the most.

Old Earl complained to the end, but he had it pretty good. I'd bet that he fished a good eighty-five of those ninety-something years. At my age, I can look forward to many more years of fishing with my family and friends. I'll count myself lucky if I can make it into my nineties before I have to sell my boat.

TWO NIGHTS IN CHILE

I wrote and submitted this short story for the Prose for Papa contest held annually at the Community Library Ernest Hemingway Festival in Ketchum, Idaho. I thought for sure I'd win the darn thing with this entry, but my dream was dashed. Hell, I never heard a word from the judges afterward. Oh well, what are you gonna do. It was fun to write nevertheless.

Jim stepped off the plane under the hot January sun in Puerto Montt and wondered if his outfitter's guide, Nico, was waiting for him.

Ideas and recurring thoughts of fishing Chile's big rivers had, until today, been just that. For too many years the timing was never right and money was elusive—always an arm's length and a publisher's promise away. He poured his heart and soul into his writing, but his books hadn't sold as well as he'd hoped. It had been five long years since a reprinting, and Jim wondered if readers were tiring of tales of fishing and wing shooting in far-off places.

Jim walked across the soft, cracked tarmac and was nearing the terminal doors when a man wearing a white-and-red flowered shirt with deep lines defining his brown face and neck quickly approached him. As he neared, the man smiled and frantically waved something back and forth overhead.

"*Jeem?*" he said. "*Teléfono, señor.*"

"Gracias." Jim took the phone and ducked under the terminal awning for relief from the heat. Listening intently to Nico's familiar voice, barely audible over the crackling and buzzing connection, Jim frowned at the news of a grounded airplane in need of repairs and Nico's missed flight from Chaitén to Puerto Montt.

Only one noon flight per day between the cities meant another overnight and less time to fish. The trip's itinerary, calling for seven days on the water, had suddenly dropped to six, and Jim wondered if this setback was a premonition of things to come.

That evening he was to fish for large rainbow trout and brown trout with Nico on the Rio Yelcho, a cold, wide, meandering river near Chaitén that wound its way through the valleys and meadows along the base of the Andes before emptying into the ocean. But even the best-laid plans can abruptly change, as they often do when traveling, and the Yelcho would have to wait until tomorrow.

Disconnecting his call, Jim offered the phone back to the man and wondered exactly where he was in Puerto Montt and where he would stay that night and if his rusty Spanish would be understood.

"¿Hay otro hotel cerca de aquí?"

"Si," the man answered, his large, straight teeth gleaming white in the noonday sun. "La Holiday Inn. It is on Costanera overlooking the harbor. Do you need the phone again?"

"You speak English," Jim said. "Thank God for that."

"Si, señor. I speak good English. You look troubled. Is the plane from Chaitén delayed?"

"Engine troubles, or so I'm told. My guide informed me the plane would arrive tomorrow. How could you tell the call came from Chaitén?" Jim said.

"You are an Americano carrying big bags and many fishing rods. People here who carry such equipment all go to Chaitén. Was that Patricio or Nico?"

"Nico," replied Jim, stooping to gather his things once again as the man stepped aside and held the terminal door open. "Do you know him?"

"Si, I know him a little. He flies here twice a month to take travelers to Yelcho Lodge. Nico is young. He will have you fishing for longer tomorrow. You will be tired when he is through with you, but you will get your pesos' worth from Nico."

Jim had stayed up far too late the night before in Santiago, sitting until the morning hours at a sidewalk café on the Plaza de Armas, listening to strolling musicians and watching dancers over fresh-baked empanadas, machas, and a bottle of inexpensive Concha y Torro merlot. The spiced meat–filled pastries and clams did little to offset the effects of the wine, and Jim felt tired today and wished his journey could continue without further delay.

Puerto Montt lacked the vibrant colors and sounds of Santiago's summer festivals and carnivals. It was a busy port of call for large cruise ships filled with wealthy tourists who did not care for the inconvenience of foreign language and culture. Jim did not delight in the thought of eating his meal that evening in the company of rich, boorish Americans and Europeans in the brightly lit hotel restaurant. He wished only to dine alone again in the open air, looking out over the water, while he drank his wine and wrote another short chapter of his book.

Jim's writing had become labored these past few years. He hoped this trip to Chile would set his pen straight again, filling his mind and body with good food, drink, fishing, and all other forms of pleasant things to write about. It is difficult to write from long-ago memories, and Jim knew that attempts to recall old feelings and conversations dulled by age did not make for good reading. The truest recollections cannot be laid down on paper unless they are written shortly after they occur.

Perhaps tomorrow things would be different. Maybe with a change of luck the plane from Chaitén would be repaired and he would meet Nico at Tepual Airport and fish the rivers he thought of so often and embark on the adventure he waited too many years to begin.

Jim was awakened the next morning to the sounds of trucks making their early-morning deliveries beneath his open hotel window. His room did not overlook the water as he had hoped. It faced east and overlooked the narrow alleyway behind the hotel that was littered with paper and cardboard and big brown dumpsters that reeked in the hot air, attracting flies and dogs.

Last evening, he'd become lost again in his writing and stayed up longer than he should have, but it could not be helped. It had been a good night for writing.

He found a table near a flower garden in a small park that overlooked the harbor. The flowers gave off a strong scent before they closed for the night, filling Jim's mind with fuzzy, wilting memories of his wedding day years ago. Carne asada and taco vendors pushed their colorful, hand-painted carts along the avenue. As the evening wore on, it was apparent and highly amusing to know that not all the tequila on one particular carne cart was used strictly for marinating the meats. As each hour passed, Jim watched the old man fill and roll his tortillas for the strolling tourists with increased flamboyance and gusto, occasionally juggling the large tortillas as they spun vertically in the air. His coordination began to wane later in the evening, and he began to drop too many onto the pavement or to tear them in two, so he stopped the juggling act. Jim imagined that the old man's wife kept a keen eye on her husband's supplies and profits. It would be hard for the vendor to explain to his wife at the end of the evening that the flour tortillas she worked hard to make every morning in her brick oven were lost to his nighttime foolishness. The vendor, looking this way and that as he picked tortillas off the dirty street, must also have realized that this unsanitary action would do nothing for his sales.

The following morning after checking out of his room, Jim ordered breakfast in the hotel's restaurant. As he sat sipping strong *café*, he thought about this trip and what he had seen and experienced during the past two days. He was here at great expense to fish for trout in the shadows of the Andes with his guide, Nico. So far, he felt like the lead character in a tragedy with a sad outcome that was all too familiar. Listening to the loud engines of the linen and garbage trucks with their brakes squealing beneath his window that morning reminded him that again, as with countless other times in his unfortunate life, his luck ran pitifully shallow and things never seemed to go as planned.

He was disappointed, but somehow he was not surprised.

A year ago, his insistence that he write and attempt to sell his writings, even through the lean years, had cost Jim his marriage. His wife of thirty years began to look on Jim and his failings as a writer with contempt and disdain. His medium was the written word, which he laboriously hammered and forged into stories. Good stories, Jim thought. But because most everybody was capable of writing, his art was nothing special in Mary's eyes. Jim was certain she would not have left him if he were a starving French impressionist who wore a felt beret. She may have even been overjoyed and proud to live a simple and frugal life in a third-floor walk-up somewhere in Paris.

The people at Yelcho Lodge knew Jim was staying at the hotel and had assured him yesterday that he'd receive confirmation of the airplane's pending noon arrival in Puerto Montt today by midmorning. It was approaching eleven thirty and he was sipping his fourth café when he felt that old sinking feeling again—today would not be his day either. Once again, something beyond his control had gone wrong.

Jim paid the hotel clerk separately for his call to the lodge. Nico's familiar voice was annoyingly pleasant as Jim listened to the situation down in Chaitén. No, the airport mechanic was not able to repair the airplane. The necessary parts would need to be ordered. Yes, they would contact the hotel as soon as the repairs were made. Two, perhaps three days at the most.

Jim's vision went white as he slammed the phone onto its cradle. He wanted to cry or scream or throw his luggage and handcrafted cane fly rods through the large plate glass window fronting the hotel. His head began to swim. How could everybody be so pleasant? His plans were quickly unraveling, and optimism suddenly left him. Thoughts of wading and fishing the Yelcho evaporated with that dying optimism, and he simply lost his will.

"¿Me pide un taxi, por favor?" Jim asked the clerk as he blinked away tears.

"Estas bien?"

"Estoy bien. Fine. I am fine. Everything is just fine. My stay here was most pleasant. A taxi. Please."

Jim's legs felt heavy as he approached the counter at Tepual Airport. The act of frantically searching his jacket pockets for money brought a bitter, defeated smile to his lips as he realized that this was the only fishing he'd do in Chile. Keeping his eyes fixed on the counter, he muttered, "Santiago, please. One way."

Jim would disembark at the Santiago airport and see yet another pleasant and pretty face behind another ticket counter. Jim would do his best to return her smile and tell her, "Cleveland, Ohio, USA. One way." Those would be the last words he would speak in Chile.

THE KINDNESS OF TIM RUSSERT

I clearly recall finishing Tim Russert's best-selling book, *Big Russ and Me*, in the summer of 2005 and thinking I might have just read the most charming, poignant, and honest book to date.

Russert wrote *Big Russ* as a tribute to his dad—Big Russ—and it chronicles Russert's 1950s upbringing in Buffalo, New York, and the lessons he learned as the son of a proud, hardworking, no-nonsense father. Big Russ, who worked for the sanitation department and also drove truck for a newspaper, was immensely proud to have served his country in WWII and provide for his family. Along the way, Big Russ made certain that his son and three daughters learned the value of hard work, honesty, humility, discipline, and faith.

The book is full of memorable personal anecdotes, and it stuck with me for days. Because I have an unwavering certainty that Russert was, at his core, a very grounded and humble person, I felt compelled to send him an email telling him how much I enjoyed his book and what it meant to me.

When I checked my email later that same day, I was delighted to see I had a message from Russert himself. Instead of having one of his staffers respond, Russert took time at the end of his busy day to write me back, telling me he was pleased to hear I enjoyed the book and asked me if I had a story to share about my dad. I wrote a story that chronicled a defining experience with my dad and sent it to Russert.

It was nearly a month later when I noticed a message from Bill Novak in my junk mail inbox. Not recognizing the name, I nearly deleted the message before I read Tim Russert's name typed on the subject line. Out of sheer curiosity, I opened the message to discover that Bill Novak was Russert's editor, and the two were collaborating to write a second book, *Wisdom of Our Fathers: Lessons and Letters from Daughters and Sons*. This book was to be a collection of stories submitted by people about their own fathers. Russert had forwarded my story to Novak, and they wished to include it in the upcoming book, due for release in the spring of 2006.

In his initial email, Novak asked me to call him in Boston, and one thing quickly led to another. Shortly after that I received a nice letter from Russert attached to a draft of my story in case I wished to change anything before Novak's final edit. Next came another call from Novak and a contract from Random House, the book publisher. (In keeping with Russert's generous nature, all of the proceeds from the sale of *Wisdom of Our Fathers* benefited the Boys & Girls Clubs of America.)

Prior to his untimely death on June 13 of this year, Russert served as NBC's senior vice president and Washington bureau chief, managing editor, and moderator of NBC's *Meet the Press*, as well as political analyst for *NBC Nightly News* and the *Today* program. He also anchored a weekly interview program on MSNBC called *The Tim Russert Show*. In addition, Russert was an attorney and member of the bar in New York and the District of Columbia.

Despite a résumé that could easily have put Russert well beyond the reach of common folks, he remained an extraordinarily grounded and humble fellow throughout his years of success and countless accolades. Those who knew him well remarked that he never forgot his middle-class Buffalo upbringing and blue-collar roots.

Despite my not knowing Russert personally, our paths did cross in 2005, and I, too, was touched by his kindness when he wrote me a couple of thoughtful emails, a letter, and a nice note on the inside cover of my copy of *Wisdom of Our Fathers*. When I pull that book from the shelf and read the note from him, I feel honored to have been a part of it. It wasn't until after his death that I discovered how truly busy Russert was day to day. I realize now how fortunate I was to have had him read my story and choose to include it in *Wisdom of Our Fathers*.

The timing of Russert's death, while tragic, was also profoundly poetic. His untimely death served as a point in time—a juncture in which we all paused to remember what is truly important in our own lives.

The most unexpected and indelible lesson Russert imparted on all of us after his passing is that we should keep our friends and family close and let them know how we feel about them before it's too late. For Mr. Russert, he expressed himself just in time.

BORN TO RIDE

The wind whistles through the vent holes of my DOT-approved helmet as I glance down at the chrome and glass speedometer on my new hog. I grin appreciatively as the bright orange needle pegs the fifty-five-miles-per-hour mark. Then I see a small black speck in the distance suddenly grow larger until, thwack! A beetle collides with my forehead. Ouch, that really hurts.

Then I hear it. Oh yeah. I twist the throttle back and tear away from the four-way stop on County Road 37 in Shafer. I do indeed hear it. I wish you could hear it, too, because it's a beautiful thing. It's a seventies funk guitar laying down a steady wacka-wacka-wacka rhythm as Isaac Hayes sings the theme from *Shaft*: "Who's the cat that won't cop out, when there's danger all about? (Shaft!) Can ya dig it?" The song is playing in my head, and I refrain from singing along out loud. No sense in drawing more attention to myself than is absolutely necessary.

Did I buy a big motorcycle? A chopper with long forks and ape-hanger handlebars? A Fat Boy, perhaps? Nah. Not my style. Instead, I bought a great-looking Yamaha Vino 125cc scooter.

I'd been seriously thinking about getting a scooter for a couple of years. I owned a Honda 150cc a number of years ago when I lived in Minneapolis, so scooting is nothing new to me. When gas prices recently surpassed the four-dollar-per-gallon mark and it began to cost eighty-five dollars to fill up the SUV, I'd had enough. Do I continue to pay around $130 each month to get to and from work driving my thirsty Isuzu Trooper, or should I get a snappy little scooter that'll sip gas and get me there and back for about twenty-five dollars per month? My wife and I didn't need to ponder those questions for very long before we decided to purchase the scooter.

I always wondered what the deal was with motorcyclists—particularly Harley riders—and that low left-handed wave they toss out to each other. After I bought the Vino and got it up to speed, I realized in short order that throwing your hand high in the air as you whiz along at sixty miles per hour on a cycle could result in your arm literally snapping in two at the elbow and whacking you repeatedly in the head. I guess there is a reason for the low wave. Another one of life's mysteries solved.

Believe it or not, I regularly get the low wave as I tool to and from work each day on the scooter. The Vino has a single chromed headlight that's quite large, so I think it fools a fair share of the Harley riders as they approach, especially when the rider is a grizzled old-timer who can't see too well to begin with.

I have mixed emotions about throwing a left hand back to these guys. I mean, would they freely and unreservedly give me the Harley brotherhood wave if they knew ahead of time they were acknowledging a middle-aged dork on a 125cc Yamaha scooter? Wearing chinos and white Jack Purcell bumper tennis shoes, no less? I seriously doubt it. I'm pretty confident about this because I actually saw a Harley rider hastily withdraw his wave after discovering I was a fraud of sorts—an ersatz biker. As we passed each other, he got a sidelong glance at my Euro-looking French bread-getter and snapped his hand back onto the handlebar so fast his arm was actually blurry. Probably wanted me to think he was smoothing out his chap or boot or something like that. In response, I let my hand hang out there for a few extra seconds, then I hit the horn a couple of times for good measure. My scooter's horn makes a high *meep-meep* sound like the *Looney Tunes'* Road Runner. I think the girlfriend on the back of his bike appreciated the humor. She smiled. I get the wave just often enough to actually believe I look sort of cool riding my scooter. I know that's not even remotely close to the truth, but a guy can dream, can't he?

One of these days I'm going to back my scooter up against the curb in front of the Border Bar in Taylors Falls, right smack in the middle of a long line of Harleys. I'll flash them the fresh press-on "Mommy" tattoo across my bicep and the custom T-shirt that reads across the back, "If you can read this, the loving wife fell off." No, I won't explain that last one to you, thank you very much. I probably wouldn't live to tell about it if I actually did those things. Funny thought, though.

The scooter is fun to drive. I forgot how good it feels to lean into a smooth curve. As an added bonus, I'm essentially thumbing my nose at Big Oil and saving a bundle of money while having all this fun. That feels pretty good too.

So when you see me out there on the highways and byways, lay that left hand of yours out there proudly. I'll toss mine right back at you, Brother.

I guess I was pretty much born to ride.

secret santa

They came for me again . . . just like last year. They knock on my office door and subject me to the same line of snippy, aggressive questioning. Usually I'm double-teamed by a couple of longtime coworkers who know me well—perhaps too well. All that's missing are the brass knuckles and truncheons.

"So, are you going to do Secret Santa again this year?" they ask. I know they're just warming up. "You don't have to, you know. Last year you were pretty crappy. Well actually, every year you're pretty crappy. So if you don't want to do it this year, that's OK. No pressure. It's just that today's the deadline and if you're going to do it, we need to know so we can add your name to the hat for the drawing. I don't know if you're aware of this or not, but people actually pray to God you don't pull their name from the hat."

Following that pitiful attempt at diplomacy, I know that the answer they'd most love to hear is, "You know, you're right. I'm not a very good Secret Santa. I think I'll pass this year." Instead, to punish them (and myself, for some strange, sadistic reason), I always cheerfully reply that yes, I'll do Secret Santa again, and this year, by gosh, I'll be the best Secret Santa ever. Ha, fat chance.

I think half the trick to the whole Secret Santa deal is to be organized and plan ahead. I know a few professional Secret Santas in our building who purchase gifts weeks in advance. My modus operandi is a bit different than that. Every year I wait for the visual reminder that the Secret Santa week has begun when I find a sack full of goodies heaped on my chair. Then I panic and run down the street to the Family Dollar, where I open my creaky wallet to buy items at an alarming rate—some of it not exactly mainstream Secret Santa stuff, if you know what I mean. Does anybody really want a three-dollar AM transistor radio with big padded earphones or a big stinky jug of Hai Karate cologne?

I'm also a tremendous failure when it comes to the annual office potluck. A few days ago, I was cornered by a hostile coworker who hissed, "You, *mein Freund*, will bring hot German potato salad this year. A lot of it. With double the bacon and onions. Every year you promise to make it and every year you fail. Bad things could happen to you if you attempt to pull any more of your shenanigans. Filling a Crock-Pot with fifteen cans of generic vegetable beef soup like you did last year ain't gonna cut it, Bucko." She stabbed the center of my chest with a stiff forefinger to emphasize the word "Bucko," so I could only assume that it wasn't an idle threat. Ouch, I had no idea Bucko was a nine-syllable word.

The other item I was expected to bring to this year's potluck was an enormous jar of pickled herring. Have you priced pickled herring lately? The store I hit this morning wanted nearly five bucks for a puny little jar of it. I don't think so. Not this year. As I quickly put the jar back on the shelf, I couldn't help but notice that the store's stinky braunschweiger logs were on sale this week. I snapped one up and made my way to the off-brand saltine crackers. Close enough for government work, I say. I calculated that the price difference would buy me three scoops of crappie minnows at my favorite bait shop, so, as far as I was concerned, the holiday food sleight of hand was a no-brainer. As an added bonus, I'm sure there will be plenty of braunschweiger and dry saltines to bring home.

seduced by a fine cane rod

I've always taken great pride in believing that I was the antithesis of fly-fishing snobbery. During the course of teaching casting lessons to lodge guests, when students invariably ask me about necessary equipment, my pat answer is something along the lines of, "It's what's between your ears that catches fish, not what's in your hand." In other words, it ain't the bamboo rods and fancy English reels that put trout in the net.

For the sake of argument, I consider the fly rod and reel to be little more than a simple fly delivery system. Of course, I must admit there is something to be said for the latent desire to cast a fly line in style. You don't need to look too long or hard to find plenty of high-end rod and reel manufacturers that offer some pretty fancy (and outrageously expensive) equipment that always sells very well. Believe me, the fly-fishing world has its fair share of hoity-toity Harris Tweed types that mumble nearly unintelligible things like, "Yes, yes . . . quite right, quite right," around pipe stems firmly clamped between their back teeth.

Last weekend, as I've done for the past five years, I worked the annual Great Waters Fly Fishing Expo at the Sheraton South in Bloomington. It's a show that puts me in contact with dozens of professionals and fly-fishing vendors from around the country and the world. We all share a passion for the sport, and many of us have become friends over the years. It's also the most effective way to advertise Seven Pines Lodge, where I instruct and guide.

A couple of years ago, the owners of the lodge commissioned Steve Pennington, an established and highly respected bamboo fly rod maker from Iowa, to build five custom-made rods for Seven Pines. On each rod blank, just above the cork handle and winding check, are the words "Seven Pines Lodge" hand-inscribed in India ink. As it turned out, the lodge could afford to purchase only four of the five rods at the time, and those four sold rather quickly to lodge guests.

As usual, this year's show was well attended and I was the only one working the Seven Pines booth, so it took me until late Saturday afternoon to venture away from my post to poke around the huge show floor and see all of the vendors. Just a couple of aisles down from my booth, I stumbled on a vendor I'd never seen before. You guessed it, Pennington Rods. I approached the Pennington booth and told the tall, older gentleman standing there, "Hello, Steve, I'm Dan Brown. I'm the guide at Seven Pines Lodge." During the course of that brief introduction, Steve Pennington's eyes grew wide and he grinned broadly as he slowly reached underneath his display table to produce a handcrafted red cedar hexagonal rod case. Steve said, "I brought this with me this weekend and hoped I'd bump into somebody from your lodge. I've had the rod for a couple of years now and I can't sell it to anybody else because it has 'Seven Pines Lodge' written on it. I'm willing to sell it to you for far less than I sold the other four. Like I said, the rod was made for you. It's the last one of five."

Holy Hannah! Talk about serendipity and karma and the Age of Aquarius and all that other hippie-dippie nonsense. Everything I thought about snotty anglers and their fancy bamboo fly rods went flying right out the window—the very window that Steve Pennington just threw open for me and me alone. What was I to do? All of a sudden I felt like Luke Skywalker. I was quickly losing my willpower as Steve smiled and pointed the rod case at me like a lightsaber, waiting for me to grasp it. The well-heeled Dark Side seduced me, and I didn't even put up a fight.

I feel like a bit of a sellout, because I did purchase that rod. But not before I asked two of the finest cane rod builders in the country to inspect and cast it. I didn't tell them what Pennington was asking for the rod. I wanted their unbiased opinions, and believe me, I know these guys well enough that they'd steer me clear of any rod that didn't pass muster, even one of their own if it didn't meet quality specs. Both of them gave the Pennington their enthusiastic seal of approval. One of those guys, my old pal Dave Norling, told me, "Dan, if you decide not to buy this rod, I will."

Maybe my long-held beliefs regarding fine bamboo fly rods stemmed from the fact that I could never afford to own one in the first place. I'm not so dense that I don't recognize a good Aesop's Fable unfolding, particularly when I'm the one playing the central character. Maybe I was that hungry fox all along, unable to reach those luscious grapes because the vine always hung a bit higher than I could reach. Well, last weekend Steve Pennington politely smiled down upon me as he bent that grapevine very low to the ground. I plucked those grapes and—lo and behold—they weren't the least bit sour. That custom-made Pennington is one sweet bamboo fly rod indeed. You see, unlike Aesop's fox, I was smart enough to never say I wouldn't eat the grapes if they were served to me on a silver platter. Yes, yes . . . quite right, quite right.

smoking fish is a family tradition

I think I picked up my smoking habit from my uncle. No, I don't mean smoking as in smoking a cigarette or cigar—I mean smoking as in smoking fish.

Growing up, my family had a cabin on Little Sand Lake near Remer, Minnesota, and next to us was my aunt and uncle's place. Each spring Uncle Dewain would smoke suckers in his brick smokehouse, located between our two cabins. I have a clear memory of aromatic woodsmoke filling the air and Dewain loading racks full of fillets into the smoker. When the fish were done a few hours later, they were a marvelous dark golden-brown color and firm to the touch. We would sit around the kitchen table with a large platter heaped with saltine crackers and smoked fillets in front of us. I also recall that it wouldn't take us very long to reduce those fillets to tidy piles of rib bones and scaly skins.

My uncle passed the fish-smoking to me, and I've been smoking fish for many years now. Like Uncle Dewain, I, too, have grown to really enjoy the process and take pride in the fish I produce. I like to mix up various brines, select just the right wood chips, and fine-tune the smoker's temperature and smoke output. It's a process and ritual that hasn't changed for thousands of years. It's one of those sublime, time-tested artisan things, like making bread or other old-world goodies like that. The art of smoking fish is transcendent and good for the soul. I guess that's why I like doing it so much.

A couple of days ago my two boys were in a mood to catch fish. They'd been after me since the morning to fish, and it seemed as if none of the other activities I offered up would scratch their itch. I suggested we walk down our bank and fish the St. Croix River and see if the suckers were running. I tied up some simple bottom rigs—#8 egg hooks and a pinch of split shot a foot or so up the line. It isn't too sophisticated, but when you thread a bit of night crawler on the hook it really does the trick on bottom feeders like suckers, carp, and the like. We poked along the bank until we found a stretch of water below a long riffle that dumped into a long rocky pool, where we found the suckers getting ready to spawn. I'll tell you what, the fish were plentiful and eager to bite. We ended up keeping around thirty fish for the smoker.

I like to smoke my fish at a lower temperature and use plenty of wood chips. After some years of smoking fish, I can honestly say that I now have the process down to something of a science. Relying on indelible memories of Uncle Dewain's smoked fish, I can turn out fish from my own smoker that look and taste just like those suckers I grew up eating in the spring of the year up at the cabin.

It's been a lot of years since I've eaten smoked sucker. I guess this year officially marks the beginning of a new spring ritual for us. Once my boys get their first taste of those fish tonight, they'll understand, like I did when I was a kid, that the effort it takes to catch, clean, and smoke spring-run suckers is worth it.

Please pass the crackers.

AUGIE AND THE BEE

I recall taking part in a spelling bee at one point in my youth. Sixth grade comes to mind, but I can't be certain. I don't remember it being that big of a deal, but I do recall that it took place in my elementary school gymnasium, and it was poorly attended. I assume I got lucky in the qualifying process, as I don't remember taking part in more than one bee.

Our two boys, Anders and August, have qualified for eight bees between them. My wife, Su, jokingly tells others that the boys got their smarts from her side of the family. Looking back, I'm quite certain this statement is anything but a joke. The more I hear it, the less I chuckle. The truth is sometimes hard to accept, and the joke is usually mentioned as a simple matter of fact.

Augie is an eighth grader this year and did take part in the Chisago Lakes District Spelling Bee on January 23. On one hand, he was proud to qualify for the bee, but on the other hand, he was somewhat reluctant to participate. By reluctant I mean that on the very day of the bee, he told his mother and me, while at the same time throwing his head back in despair, "I don't want to be in the bee! Do I have to be in the bee?!" Maybe *reluctant* isn't the right word. *Horrified*? To Augie's way of thinking, it is hard to be a cool eighth grader while sharing a stage at a public venue with sawed-off fifth graders who could very well destroy him in a spell-off. Thank goodness his good friend and classmate Zach Walden also participated in the bee. They might get destroyed, but they would get destroyed together, which, to an eighth-grade boy, is somehow acceptable and cool.

There are a lot of factors that determine whether a kid will advance from one round to the next in a spelling bee. The first is the flop-sweat factor. This occurs when a speller is suddenly overwhelmed by bright lights, a microphone, steely-eyed judges, tomb-like silence, and the resulting uncertainty of whether the word *car* begins with the letter *C* or *K*. This always happens in the first or second round to at least one speller. After hearing the judge say, "That is incorrect," the young dejected speller takes a seat alongside the other kids with a shell-shocked look on his or her face. I don't know, maybe the kid heard one too many Kars4kids.org radio spots—"K-A-R-S: Kars4Kids."

Another factor is simply word recognition. One of the words in the later rounds of the bee was *gendarme*. As in French police officer. If your parents didn't feed you a fairly steady nighttime reading diet of *Madeline* books, you would not be in a very good position to correctly spell this word, particularly if the word is pronounced correctly. The *zh* sound in French is a killer, as the boy who was expected to spell this word found out in short order.

I recorded a short video for Facebook just before the bee got underway. I told folks to watch for a few things regarding young Augie and his progress—or lack thereof—during the bee. If he asked to have the word repeated, he was in pretty good shape. If he asked to have the word used in a sentence, still in fairly decent shape. But if Augie asked for the language of origin, I told viewers, "It's all over, Johnny. He has no clue what the word is, let alone how to spell it." This fact is doubly true if the word originated from a dead language like Latin. I can't be certain, but there must be a reason why a language undergoes what is known as language death. Maybe the language was full of stupid words nobody could spell.

I also mentioned in the video that if a skinny little fifth grader takes the stage wearing a bow tie, watch out. If roman numerals III or IV follow his name, forget about it. This usually means the boy's mom and/or dad is an attorney. These are the children whose folks make a living from the precise use and spelling of words, and that spells T-R-O-U-B-L-E for the rest of our kids. The big shiny trophy could safely be handed to the well-heeled child in the bow tie before the bee even gets underway, but convention must be followed, I guess.

Su and I have changed our approach to these spelling bees with the boys over the years. Anders won the bee as a fifth grader, due in large part to the fact that we insisted he study properly for it. He enjoyed it too. We think. Night after night, he would pore over the dictionary with gusto, his sharpened number two pencil scratching and skittering across a spiral notebook. We even had the boys watch *Akeelah and the Bee*, a sort of a geeky pump-up movie to help motivate would-be spelling bee champs. We've come to the realization that qualifying for a district spelling bee is an honor in and of itself, so our insistence that the boys break out the dictionary has waned quite a bit in subsequent years. I asked Augie on the evening of the last bee, "So, how much did you study for the bee?" He replied, "About fifteen minutes in the van." Hey, good enough for me.

Augie made it to within one correct spelling of reaching the regional qualifying round. The word *criterion* tripped him up, but he did spell *remonstrance* correctly the round before. He even asked for the language of origin, which is French and medieval Latin, and he somehow managed to spell it correctly. So much for my theory.

I was delighted when a fifth-grade girl won this year's bee. Her winning word was *au fait*, which means to have a good or detailed knowledge of something. She was required to spell one last word to clinch the title, but it was *au fait* that left her as the lone speller at the end of the evening. Very impressive indeed. Augie might've been able to spell the word *parfait*, as he does possess a detailed knowledge of a Dairy Queen menu board, but it turned out that the evening ended on a perfect note. Any kid who honestly knows how to spell *au fait* deserves the victory.

A BOY'S FIRST PHEASANT HUNT

Thinking back to when you were twelve years old, what do you remember most? What events took place at that time of your life that became so indelibly inked in your memory that you recall them with crystal clarity? I remember my first pheasant hunt down near Gaylord and Pipestone, Minnesota, with my dad, uncles, and grandpa, and the fond memory of that trip is as clear in my mind as if it happened just yesterday.

I now have a son who is twelve years old, and one thing I didn't want to see come and go this year was an opportunity for my boy Anders to experience his own first pheasant hunt with his dad and grandpa. But thoughts of the time and expense of a long road trip out to western Minnesota or the Dakotas pushed me to consider options closer to home. A few weeks ago, after careful internet research and reading various reviews of nearby hunting preserves and clubs, I chose to give Wings North a call. Wings North is located just outside of Pine City and would allow Anders, his grandpa Ron, and me the chance to experience a quality pheasant hunt together, all within the span of an afternoon.

I hadn't done any preserve hunting before and didn't know what to expect. Chad Hughes, owner of Wings North, simply explained that "every day is like opening day." Like I said, I'd never hunted at a place where you pay for birds. For some reason, I had visions of birds just standing around in an open field, waiting around somewhat stupidly for their unfortunate fate.

Anders holding some roosters after a beautiful day of hunting pheasants at Wings North near Pine City, Minnesota. The golden late-day sun and Anders's smile in this photo pretty much say it all. A memorable day indeed.

Well, my preconceived notion of a hunting preserve could not have been further from the truth. Yes, birds are released prior to the time you take to the fields, but the birds we hunted at Wings North were anything but stupid. They behaved just like any other pheasants I've encountered in the wild, hunkering down in heavy cover and holding tight until our guide's dog sniffed them out. Any ideas of what others unfairly refer to as a "canned hunt" evaporated very quickly. The birds burst from the tall grass in a flurry of wing beats and cackles and iridescence, and we as hunters were afforded no more advantage than the birds we hunted. Ron, Anders, and I needed to be sharp and swing our guns true if we were to hit any birds, and I'm happy to report that we all shot pretty well that afternoon.

Anders, having never shot a game bird prior to this trip, impressed Ron and me and our guide, Dave, with a shot of about forty yards. Watching Anders shoot, I was heartened to see that he didn't just throw the butt of the gun against his shoulder and snap off a shot. He swung the gun's barrel on a good plane, led the rooster as it quartered away, and was rewarded with the sight of a bird neatly folding its wings and falling back to earth. It was evident that he had been listening to what I'd been trying to teach him about wing shooting. We shot a total of ten pheasants that afternoon, with Anders taking credit for three birds. I was quite proud of his performance that day.

Anders's first pheasant hunt, like my own and his grandpa's before that, will no doubt be burned in his memory and fondly remembered for the rest of his life. I took a number of good photographs chronicling that historic day. The late afternoon sun, not long before it touched the horizon, cast a soft, golden light that shone on a timeless image: a smiling boy, his shotgun cradled under his arm, proudly holding a number of colorful roosters

DON'T BELIEVE EVERYTHING a FISHERMAN TELLS YOU

There is a time-honored and well-founded belief that fishermen are filthy liars. And it is true that this belief is based entirely on fact. I'm not singling out the men, either. Female anglers are very capable of glibly fibbing with the best of them.

When the ice leaves our lakes and rivers, it's the time of year when watercooler talk turns to fishing, particularly for ice-out crappies and walleyes. Just the other day I nonchalantly asked a nice gal I know where she's planning to do her spring crappie fishing. She's a very good crappie angler and always does well during the month of April. I had already heard from her blabby friend and fishing partner last week where they intended to fish, so I knew the answer before I asked the question. Guess what? That seemingly honest gal looked me dead in the eyes and flat-out lied to me. Wow, talk about an Oscar-worthy performance. She'd have no trouble beating a lie-detector test. Her husband better stay on her good side. "Who, Bill? He left for the office just like he does every morning. That's right, officer. Why, is he missing?"

This morning I received an email from a guy I know who tried (very slyly, I might add) to rattle the back door for useful information. Usually, the backdoor question is cleverly hidden somewhere between the salutation, "Hi, good buddy," and the heartfelt closing, "Your best fishin' pal of all time."

Along with the covert backdoor question, in which the questioner attempts to pickpocket information from some gullible dope, there is also the overt frontal-assault technique. These are two very distinct methods of operation, but both are equally effective if performed properly.

The frontal-assault method is intended to momentarily stun the fellow angler—usually in a public setting, like a bait shop—causing him to lose focus and the ability to lie. The presence of other anglers in the room forces pride to creep into the equation, and the guy being asked the questions usually tells the truth. I've seen it happen, and it ain't pretty. Once the truth is out, it is immediately recognized as being the truth. Anglers have well-honed senses and can smell a truth a mile away.

When it comes to either withholding information (lying by omission) or simply sending a fellow angler to Timbuktu to get skunked on a crummy lake, I can be a most persuasive liar. Hey, it's tough out there. You need to use your best poker face and keep your cards close to your vest. When somebody has you under a hot bulb and is sweating you for information, swallow your pride and keep good spots to yourself. After all, it took some hard work on your part to wheedle the spots you do have from honest schmucks in the first place. If you tip your hand and allow others to get a good look at your cards, believe me, you can kiss those secret hot spots goodbye.

Where am I heading for crappies this week, you ask? Let me think about that for a moment before I answer.

THINGS I SHOULD'VE LEARNED AS A KID

i'm not very handy when it comes to fixing things. My older brother, on the other hand, is quite capable of doing pretty much any plumbing or electrical work, because he actually took the time to learn from our dad when we were growing up. I didn't like learning from Dad. It certainly wasn't any fun. "Hold this. No, not like that! Like this! Gimme that thing! Goddamn it! What the hell's the matter with you?!"

It was that sort of behavior from my dad that pushed me to become passive-aggressive at a very early age. To survive, I quickly learned to take on the rotten-helper role. I'd point the flashlight at the back of Pop's head while he was underneath the sink skinning his knuckles on a leaky trap in the pitch dark. Then, after he'd cuss and clank his head on a pipe while extricating himself from underneath the cabinet to give me the what for, I'd scald his left retina with the beam. *Zzzzap!* Whoops, my bad. Hope you don't need to drive the car anytime soon.

For goodness' sake, with all that yelling and negativity going on, it's no wonder I still can't change a light bulb without hearing a symphony of ruinous self-talk in my head. I thought I'd give you a glimpse into my past, because to this day—I'm forty-three years old—I'm still pretty much worthless when it comes to home improvement.

This year for Christmas, our hot water heater gave up the ghost. I suppose it was the equivalent of Santa leaving me a lump of coal in my stocking. Probably payback for being an inattentive smart-ass kid all those years ago. Anyway, I found myself once again at the mercy of my dad's infinite "how-to" wisdom and gave him a call for help. I thought about calling a friend or a brother-in-law first, but this sort of job required a helper with a sense of forced obligation that only a direct bloodline relative could provide. The first words out of his mouth were, "Hell, all you need to do is sweat a coupla joints and wire in your 220. You've sweated pipes before, ain'tcha?" Speaking of sweat, I felt some begin to pop out on my forehead. I felt like I was twelve years old all over again as I feebly replied, "Uh . . . well . . . no, not exactly. The last time our water heater blew up, Brad Guggisberg—you remember Brad—anyway, he came over and helped me. He's like me, except he listened to his dad growing up. Heh-heh."

Anyway, Dad eventually showed up at the house later that day with his propane torch, flux, roll of solder, and pipe cutter. He had to ask me the questions he'd been dying to ask since he left his place in Golden Valley an hour earlier: "You mean to tell me you still ain't learned nuttin' after thirty years? You know what a plumber gets an hour? Huh? Them bums'll charge you an hour's labor just for showing up! Your trouble is, you'd rather go fishing than learn how to be handy. Rubbing copper pipes with a frozen crappie ain't gonna give you hot water, son."

I didn't have the heart to tell him that, after all these years, I still didn't give a rat's ass about flux and solder and sweating pipes. Besides, I know some plumbers, and not all of them are bums. And to top it all off, for years now I've made some pretty respectable dough taking folks fishing. Instead, for his sake, I hung my head in a close approximation of shame and at the same time smiled and wondered where I put that new super-bright LED flashlight of mine.

we will have a good time, even if it kills us

I'm beginning to fall into the somewhat misguided habit of looking for what I perceive to be good smallmouth water north of Taylors Falls, Minnesota. I'm not talking about running up the river a little ways, mind you. Heck no, that'd be too easy. Short trips give me the diluted notion that I somehow didn't work and plan hard enough to catch fish. No, I'm talking about distances that compel me to check the truck's dipstick and tire pressure before heading out and require at least one pit stop for a bathroom break and snacks. I'm beginning to think that with today's fuel prices, this habit could seriously affect the bank account.

My buddy Paul Bury and I did a two-day float down the upper reaches of the St. Croix a couple of weeks ago. With our busy work and family lives, we settled on the only two days that would fit our hectic schedules. We'd been planning this trip for a few months, and as our trip date drew nearer, I'd been crossing my fingers while checking the ten-day forecast. The weather was shaping up to be potentially pretty dicey, and it looked as though we wouldn't get through this thing without breaking out the foul-weather gear. You know how it goes—you pen some dates on the kitchen calendar and there they remain, indelibly inked, because the rest of your schedule won't allow them to budge.

We put in at Norway Point Landing on a Sunday afternoon, and it didn't take long for the thunder, lightning, high winds, and Old-Book-of-Genesis-type rain to begin. Soaked to the bone as I attempted to oar my personal pontoon craft against the stiff southerly wind, I half expected to look to the shoreline and see an old-timer in flowing robes hammering together a big wooden boat.

The fun didn't end there. Luckily for us, the torrential down-pour was still in full swing as we beached our crafts at the campsite (which we nearly overshot due to the quickly fading light). Instead of pitching a cozy camp under the stars and enjoying a meal of freshly caught fish around the open fire, we found ourselves run-ning south on County Road F into Grantsburg, Wisconsin, wipers on full tilt, for frozen pizza and flat domestic tap beer at a local watering hole. Later on, the pizza wasn't settling too well with my insides as Paul closed the back hatch of his vehicle for the night . . . from the inside. Yes, the rain and our string of bad luck contin-ued well into the evening, forcing us to sleep in the back end of his midsize SUV. The loud, incessant *ping-ping-ping-ping-ping* of fat raindrops hammering the roof a scant couple of feet above my head finally lulled me to sleep just before I almost lost my mind. When we awoke, my legs and hips were numb from attempting to stretch out my six-foot frame in a space that this particular ve-hicle manufacturer boasts to be sixty-six inches long. If I were a half foot shorter, I would've been in terrific shape that morning.

On Monday afternoon, we took out at the Highway 70 bridge in Grantsburg not long after the weather changed for the better. Sure, we caught fish and had fun, but I'd admit now that it was a forced kind of fun. The kind of fun and high spirits you're forced to muster up during a miserable fishing trip as you tell yourself, "By God, we will have a good time, even if it kills us." We couldn't change our trip dates and Mother Nature dealt us a less-than-ideal weather hand. Not much you can do about that, I guess.

A few evenings ago, I stepped down to the bank of the St. Croix River near our home in Taylors Falls. I immediately noticed that the river just below the house is darn near as pretty as the same river fifty miles north. And, believe it or not, the smallies look remarkably like the smallies fifty miles north. They doggedly fight and put the same bend on my fly rod too.

It takes me about three minutes to get from my front door to dipping my toes in the river. No pit stops, no high-priced gas, no packing, and no driving. Maybe I should get back into the habit of enjoying what's right under my nose. If it begins to rain while I'm fishing below the house, it's a short hike up the bank to hot food and a warm, soft bed.

THE 16-gauge: DARLING OF THE UPLAND HUNTER

For a number of years, I've had my heart set on carrying a 16-gauge for upland birds. It's still considered a nostalgic bore, a gun that brings to mind old black-and-white photos of quail hunters wearing fedoras, corduroy-collared field jackets, and tall lace-up boots. Setting aside the nostalgia and the aesthetics, there is strong evidence to suggest that the 16-gauge is an extremely effective bore, and I've always been puzzled as to why I don't see more of them afield. With its bore diameter of .662 inches, it falls nearly smack-dab in the middle of the 12-gauge (.730 inches) and 20-gauge (.615 inches) and, to my way of thinking, represents the best of both worlds and the most versatile gun to handle just about anything that flies.

There was always one hurdle that prevented me from thinking too seriously about owning a sixteen, and that was the price. It was never a mystery to me why 16-gauge guns were typically far more expensive than their 12- and 20-gauge counterparts. The fact of the matter is that there's a fairly limited demand for this bore, and gun manufacturers spend quite a bit of money to create and calibrate the machinery necessary to turn out a relative few of them.

Another compelling reason to carry a 16-gauge has to do with its inherent ballistics. In my never-ending online quest for information about sixteens, I found a great website—The 16 Gauge Society—which devotes all of its energy to the discussion of 16-gauge guns, manufacturers, ammunition, ballistics, and wing shooting. At this site, I found the following explanation of the sixteen's ballistics and how it uniquely throws shot:

A larger shot charge does not make a small bore better. The advantages of a 16-gauge over a 20 bore are more about ballistics than weight, although they are close in weight also. A 16-gauge, at a .662-inch bore, is ballistically pure with a 1-ounce shot charge. This means that 1 ounce of shot pours down a bore of that size with minimal "shot stringing." This results in the shot swarm arriving at the target at virtually the same time. Forcing too large a charge down a smaller bore—the same 1 ounce or more in a 20-gauge for instance—can result in a shot string of several feet or more and limits the number of pellets with a chance of intercepting a fast moving target. A 16-gauge with 1 ounce of shot has plenty of pellets and a near perfect pattern.

I agree that was a bit wordy, but I couldn't explain it any better. My dream of owning a 16-gauge remained just that until fairly recently. Late in the spring I discovered that the Browning Arms Company offered special below–dealer price discounts to members of the Outdoor Writers Association of America. As a member of that organization, this pleased me to no end. However, I knew enough (or so I thought) about Browning's line of shotguns to know that they didn't manufacture a 16-gauge. One trip to their website proved I was wrong. Browning did manufacture a very limited number of BPS (that is, Browning Pump Shotgun) sixteens for the shotgun industry's Shot Show. They produced a 16-gauge Hunter and a 16-gauge Upland Special. I came to discover that only 265 Upland Specials (differentiated from the Hunter by its straight English stock) were produced with a twenty-six-inch barrel.

Of course, the Upland Special with the twenty-six-inch barrel was the gun I wanted to get my hands on in the worst way.

Back in May I talked with a Browning representative at the corporate headquarters about the possibility of finding and purchasing this gun. He informed me that all of the Uplands were sold at the shot show to a very select number of dealers, but he also said that anything can happen and he would keep an eye out for any dealer that'd be willing to cancel their order.

I'm happy to say that my Browning rep kept me in mind during those interim months and called me just a couple of days ago. He informed me that the impossible happened—he found a dealer with an extra BPS Upland Special 16-gauge. And if that wasn't enough good news for one day, he told me that my OWAA discount could be applied to the sale of this gun.

Now all I have to do is wait for it to be delivered to my local FFL dealer. The rep told me delivery could take a couple of weeks or possibly as long as a month. To be honest, I can barely wait to put that 16-gauge to use in the woods and fields.

I wonder if I still have that old musty corduroy-collared field jacket down in the basement somewhere?

A GOOD PORCH

I light the gas heater in the back porch of our house after my wife and I get the boys settled into their beds. Our house, filled with sounds of talk, laughter, music, and squeaking floorboards during the day, becomes quiet and serene during the evening hours.

On the porch, during the last hour or two of the day, I can enjoy a good book or tie some smallmouth poppers or trout flies. This night, as I carefully wind dubbing and feathers onto a small hook, my mind takes me to familiar waters on a warm spring day and I see trout rise.

Sitting at my fly-tying table, my eyes are drawn to the items that adorn the walls and shelves in the porch: fly rods and reels, Kromer caps, antique barometers, German steins, wooden snowshoes, an upland vest, numerous deer antlers, and framed photographs. Many of these personal items invoke vivid and indelible memories that comfort me. Other items picked up along the way somehow seem to deserve a prominent spot somewhere in the porch.

Some would argue there is too much stuff in our porch, and to those who would make that statement, they'd be right—to a point. To those folks, the old porch is indeed filled with stuff. But stuff is funny. I keep it around and cherish it when the mere sight of it brings to mind memories of good or pleasant times. I see objects and artifacts that commemorate a lifetime of experiences. I have a story to tell about most of the stuff you'd find in our porch.

Our black lab, Ned, smells something interesting wafting beneath the door to the kitchen and moans as he gets up off the floor. The floor of the porch isn't properly insulated and can become quite drafty, so we always close the two doors that connect the porch to the main house to keep the cold at bay. Ned looks over his shoulder at me and waits patiently as I get up to let him out. When I open the door, I can smell it too; something is baking. I can also faintly hear Tony Bennett sing a bouncy tune about picking a plum and how the best is yet to come.

The rustic porch was built in the late 1950s and juts from our house like an architect's afterthought. Our house is an 1869 Italianate listed as the John Daubney House on the National Register of Historic Places, so the porch really was an afterthought. The knotty pine walls, darkened with age, and Berber carpeting contrast sharply with the formality of the main house. But to be honest, I can't fathom why it took nearly a century for someone to wise up and add a porch onto the back of our house. I couldn't imagine the house without it, as it truly does balance the mood of the place.

The old porch has a good personality that radiates a warmth all its own, even on those cold fall and winter days and nights. The collectibles decorating the walls give the space the feel and patina of a gentleman's lodge. I like our porch. It's far from perfect, with a couple of water-stained ceiling tiles and ill-fitting windows, but it's comfortable, like a favorite chair, and I like it nevertheless. It's a good porch.

ALL i want for christmas

There was a time in my life (probably more years than I care to admit) when I wanted stuff—oh man, did I want stuff, and lots of it. When asked what I wanted for Christmas, the question alone nearly sent my head reeling with the limitless possibilities. Jeez, what didn't I want? Of course, "want" and "need" are entirely different concepts, but for a lifelong outdoor junkie with a serious jones for anything on the market that promised I'd catch more fish or shoot more birds and deer, the two words were irrevocably the same.

Thankfully, there comes a time in your life when a healthy dose of skepticism and cynicism sets in—middle age, I think—and you're finally able to see through all the marketing BS for what it is. In one of the outdoor publications I receive every couple of weeks, I recently read an advertisement for special doe-in-estrus urine that goes for thirty-five dollars a bottle. I thought, "Well, for that price, it better be one big ol' jug of pee. Probably delivered by FedEx and wheeled to my doorstep on a hand truck." I had to hold the page an arm's length away to make out the fine print stating that this magical "Eau d'Estrus" is bottled one ounce at a time. Unless my decimal's in the wrong place, that works out to $4,480 per gallon. Whew, prices like that for bodily waste make you forget all about high gas prices, don't they? For that kind of money, a guy would be tempted to keep a couple of deer in the backyard parked in front of a big water trough. I can just hear it now: "Deer pee? You paid thirty-five bucks for one ounce . . . of deer pee?!" Part of me (the stupid part) was secretly tempted to order a bottle. You know, just to see if every lovestruck buck in the county would come blindly running to its pungent, sexy fragrance. It was probably a good thing for me—and my marriage—that I decided against that purchase. I'd just wind up spilling it in the back end of the truck or allowing it to freeze solid and blow the plastic screw cap, just like every other bottle of deer urine I've mistreated. Believe me, you don't want to smell the inside of my truck at the moment.

I see that similar marketing shenanigans have also infiltrated the world of ice fishing. Last year, the big deal was ice fishing rods that vibrate and buzz at the flip of a switch. Oh yeah, that's precisely what I need—another gizmo in my life with an insatiable appetite for expensive alkaline batteries. I thought I read somewhere that prolonged exposure to vibrations can cause musculoskeletal disorders. I get out ice fishing enough that I'd probably develop one of these disorders if I hung on to a vibrating fishing rod all day. If that weren't enough, this season's trickery includes a particular tip-up that gobbles up D-cell batteries at the rate of two every twelve hours to electronically jig your bait. You get the impression that somewhere there's a roomful of fishing tackle and battery big shots sealing deals, sipping champagne, and having a good laugh at our expense.

See what I'm getting at? It's exhausting. I can't keep up with this stuff anymore. It took me a couple of years to get on board with phosphorescent glow jigs and the tiny fifteen-dollar single-bulb flashlight you need to make the jigs glow. The little flashlights are so small that I manage to lose anywhere between three and five of them every season. And the LED bulb throws off such an intense light that you'd better be sure you're not pointing it in the wrong direction when that sucker goes off. One misdirected shot in the eyeballs will render you dazed and useless for the remainder of the evening's fishing trip.

Even if buzzing rods and jigging tip-ups do work and are all the rage, the skeptic in me is resisting the purchase of these new-fangled items. I don't need more electronic gizmos this year for Christmas, and I don't like the idea that my success on the ice depends on whether I have a limitless supply of fully juiced batteries. At the rate things are going, I'd have to lug a case of batteries around with me everywhere I go.

This Christmas I made things easy on everybody. I'm actually wearing this year's present as I write this column. I bought it myself. It's a heavy wool shirt jacket made up in Bemidji, Minnesota. Green-and-black plaid. Very nice. If denying myself state-of-the-art equipment means more fishless days, well, by God, I'm gonna look good when I get skunked.

Keep a Packers Cap Handy

I've been touting the great fishing on lakes in and around Chisago County and in east-central Minnesota for years now, but I'd be remiss if I didn't let you in on a little secret. For as little as fifty dollars you can purchase an annual, nonresident Wisconsin angling license to include Sconnie's many productive lakes and rivers in your fishing repertoire.

I suppose that for some Minnesotans, the thought of fishing across the border violates some sort of deeply infused, self-righteous canon formulated by watching too many Vikings-Packers battles, but I can assure you, the fish bite just the same on the east of the St. Croix River. That's right, the fish couldn't care less what team you root for.

A couple of years ago, a coworker of mine turned me on to a lake outside of Eureka that has been my go-to water for big—and I mean big—sunfish and crappies ever since. Some very reputable muskie lakes, including Deer Lake just east of St. Croix Falls, produce large fish each year, and walleye anglers enjoy consistent success on numerous Polk and Burnett County lakes. A leisurely drive south on Wisconsin Highway 35 will put you on the Willow, Kinnickinnic, and Rush Rivers, three blue-ribbon trout fisheries.

Once you're in Wisconsin, it's pretty cool to read roadside billboards and signs advertising nearby lodges and supper clubs abundant in the northern third of the state. Thousands of anglers and vacationers from Milwaukee, Chicago, and other points south make northern Wisconsin their destination each year. Depending on where you live in Minnesota, you're probably no more than a thirty-minute drive from this "up north" experience.

Here are a few tips when you do decide to fish Wisconsin waters. As tough as it sounds, swallow your Purple Pride and stow a beat-up Packers cap in the back seat of your vehicle. Screw it on your head before you hit a Wisconsin bait shop and gripe to the guy scooping minnows that the Pack nearly gave you a heart attack on Sunday. This is the tough part, but offering up a simple, "Yah, well, da Vikes and da Bears still suck, dat's for sure," is always a safe bet too. Whether the Packers won or lost that week is irrelevant. Flaming the Vikings and Bears seems to always do the trick, and it's sure to get Wisconsin folks talking freely. Once you do that, finding out where the fish are biting should be a snap.

The guy in the bait shop ringing up your minnows and Flu Flu Jigs may not be wearing a foam rubber wedge of cheese on his head, but it's a good bet that he watches a lot of Packers football.

A Timeless Rite of Passage

It never fails to happen when you take kids ice fishing. You tell the little urchins over and over to be careful and mindful of where they walk, and yet, despite repeated warnings, it happens— the excited and inattentive youngster steps into a hole drilled in the ice and does a spot-on impersonation of the Wicked Witch of the West, slowly twisting and clawing at the air before the lake claims his or her entire leg.

Proving this time-tested theory, it happened yet again last week, just as I knew it would. The surface of the ice where we fished had more holes in it than a Lite-Brite board, so you could say that I was kind of expecting it to happen. Actually, it's a wonder it only occurred once that afternoon, and more surprisingly, that it took my four-year-old nephew, John, such a long time to finally get wet. A long time by these standards anyway. I believe that he remained dry for all of ten minutes before the unfortunate and uncomfortable incident.

"Uncle Dan! Uncle Dan! Um, is it alright if I . . . *Aaaarrgh!*" His body lurched sideways like the Leaning Tower of Pisa and down he went. John's dad, Mark, was savvy enough to act as if soaking a leg in thirty-three-degree water was simply part of the whole ice fishing process—a rite of passage of sorts.

Lacking any fanfare, Mark simply took John into the fish house, where he dumped a fair amount of water from a boot, wrung a few things out, lined the boot with a plastic bag, and swapped the wet sock for a dry one. Smart thinking, because the moment a kid with a wet leg believes that his limb might freeze solid and possibly snap clean off, your well-planned afternoon of fishing is shot.

Yes, the ol' leg-in-the-hole deal is pretty traumatic and has abruptly ended countless ice fishing trips. Somehow, it always seems to occur precisely between the time you've invested drilling holes and when you can actually sit down to fish and enjoy the fruits of your labor.

I'm convinced that a kid—any kid—could somehow find a single hole drilled in a five-hundred-acre lake and come limping back with a soggy boot full of water to prove it.

It's just one of those cosmic things that may never be fully explained.

A STUDY IN STUPIDITY

As I lay on my back in the slushy, wet snow, gazing up at the beautiful azure sky, my first thought was, *Yes, I did it.* Then I looked down to discover my skis were no longer attached to my ski boots. I had double ejected, which, when snow skiing, is never a good thing.

OK, time to back up a bit and rethink this: What exactly *did* I do? I was feeling a bit disoriented, so I remained somewhat motionless in the snow and took a quick inventory of my physical state, all the while thoroughly enjoying the pretty blue sky. I thought I heard birds singing but came to realize we don't have any winter songbirds in the area whose call is *Holy-shit-did-you-see-that?!* *Holy-shit-did-you-see-that?!* I continued to review the sequence of events that led to this failure of epic proportion, trying to determine what exactly went wrong.

While standing at the top of the run, it had taken some time to convince my two boys that I could in fact ski over the standing water and make it unscathed to the other side of the pond. (We were at Wild Mountain for the annual spring-thaw Slush Fest, so the standing water at the bottom of a ski run was intentional.) My oldest son, Anders, who was very skeptical from the get-go, later told me I was going way too fast. "Dad," he said, "you were going like fifty miles an hour when you hit the water." Sort of a stretch, but I got the point. I did ski across the water—successfully I might add, as evidenced by my dry ski boots and ski pants—but the plan hit the fan when I failed to keep my weight back and hop up onto the snow at the far end of the pond. Witnesses later told me my ski tips slammed into the vertical bank of icy snow, causing the immediate double ejection, which, in turn, sent me cartwheeling through the air. I do remember making a loud *OOOF!* sound when I landed flat on my back against the hardpack and slid a number of feet to a merciful stop.

My two boys are accomplished aerialists, both on a trampoline and in the terrain park on their skis. I do know that when a body spins forward or backward, there are certain degrees that are good, and there are others that are bad. If you're doing a front or back flip, 360 degrees is good, because you land on your feet or skis. What I nailed on Saturday, after being violently ripped from my skis, was a 270. That, of course, is not nearly as good, because a 270 on skis can cause broken bones, internal bleeding, and head injury. See the difference? As I was spinning like a rag doll, I do recall the snow rushing perilously close to my face and thinking, *OK, I got this. I'm clearly at 180, so if I tuck right now, I can fully rotate and land a 360.* But these days, my body isn't exactly able to tuck on command, so I wound up 90 degrees shy of ideal.

Every once in a while, I have a hard time coming to terms with my chronological age. When I suffer periods of temporary insanity, as I clearly did last Saturday, I attempt to do things my body simply cannot do any longer. As my wife, Su, gently reminded me after witnessing my cartoon-like double ejection on the ski slope: "ARE YOU INSANE! YOU'RE ALMOST FIFTY [insert favorite f-word expletive here] YEARS OLD!"

Just last summer I attempted a backflip on the kids' trampoline in our backyard. The result of that lapse of judgment turned out roughly the same way as the skiing incident, except in reverse. I landed on my stomach and my bare shins slammed against the galvanized steel outer frame of the trampoline—*CLANK!* Steel versus bone. When the blinding-white pain eventually subsided and I could actually see, I looked down and half expected to find my lower legs and feet snapped off and lying on the ground.

I bring up the trampoline story because there is clearly a pattern here. When will I learn? When will I listen to others once they strongly recommend I not attempt some cockamamie, half-baked stunt like I pulled last Saturday? Boy, I hope it's soon. These epic failures are beginning to take a toll on me.

A Great Day For Sledding

A friend of ours said to my wife the other day, "*Another* fishing article?" Ouch, that hurt. Jeepers, that's what I do, you know, write about fishing and hunting. Then I got to thinking that perhaps she's right and reminded myself that my weekly newspaper column, Discovering the Outdoors, leaves quite a bit of leeway and latitude for countless other outdoor pursuits.

Last Saturday, while my wife was coaching a ski race at Trollhaugen, the boys and I ventured up the road to do some sledding with our friends at Wild River State Park. It was a mild day with bright sunshine, and the fresh snow we received the night before made for perfect conditions to be outside playing with the kids. To be perfectly honest, I haven't had that much fun in quite a while.

Momentarily forgetting my age and physical state, I was tempted once or twice to try the run-and-jump start. You know the one. You run downhill while holding the flimsy, cracked plastic sled at your side; propel yourself headfirst into the air (à la Pete Rose); tuck the sled beneath you; and make a crushing stomach landing on the hard-packed snow. The only thing preventing me from attempting this feat was the realization that the slippery roads might impede the EMS from arriving at the crash site and attending to my extensive injuries in a timely manner.

I learned that you don't need to find a hill as steep and long as K2 to have a good time. In the eyes of little kids who stand only a few feet tall, just about any hill looks pretty impressive. And when you do head for a hill with the youngsters in tow, don't expect to do "a little sledding." I learned that on Saturday too. It took a fair amount of cajoling and promises of hot chocolate and cookies to pry the boys' cold hands from their sleds and get them headed for the truck. They're masterful sulkers and nearly had me feeling crummy about calling it quits, but they did finally concede without incident. If they had had their way, and if it weren't for trivial things like sleeping and eating, they'd probably still be out there.

I really enjoy fishing, but I won't hesitate to tell you that bombing a well-groomed hill with my two boys beats the heck out of catching crappies any day. Yes, I'll admit, even when the crappies are really biting.

Tempting Fate with a Fly Rod

Over the years I've become pretty good at making bad decisions with a fly rod in my hand. This past September, on a day nearing the end of the trout season, I experienced just such an occasion: I hooked—and lost—what could've been the largest brown trout I've seen in a number of years.

What I can't seem to get through my head is the fact that some decisions I make just beg to tempt fate. And if fate does decide to make an appearance, I usually wind up holding a fly rod that was—a mere moment earlier—attached to a really big fish. I then begin to swear like a merchant marine, and my hands shake so badly that I can't tie on another fly to save my life. When I lose big fish, and thankfully it isn't all that often, I tend to devolve rather quickly, and it isn't a pretty sight. Like "the Old Man" in *A Christmas Story*, I weave a tapestry of obscenities I am quite certain hang for a long time over southeastern Minnesota.

This particular tragedy began when a good friend of mine, Bill Hinton, suggested I fish Crow Springs, a feeder creek of the Whitewater River near Elba, Minnesota. Trout Unlimited had done some work on the stream, and the fishing there was supposed to be good. Fishing new water is always appealing, so I made the trip down to fish a stretch of water nicely enhanced with lunker structures (undercut banks) and limestone riprap (boulders added to the banks to prevent erosion).

The term *lunker structure* should've been the tip, but I chose to ignore it. It was a pretty dinky stream, and I foolishly thought, *C'mon, how big could the fish in here be?* At home I have a fiberglass reproduction of a twenty-four-inch brown trout I caught in a ribbon of water narrow enough to pee across, so you could say my initial thought about fish size was the first bad decision of the day.

The next decision I made actually gave me pause as I was making it. Prior to fishing, I stood next to the stream and decided to tie on a #8 Dave's Hopper. This is a big, sexy grasshopper pattern that'll turn the heads of trout everywhere grasshoppers are present. Every once in a while, particularly on a windy day, a grasshopper will misjudge a hop and splat helplessly onto the surface of the water. When this happens, the life expectancy of that hopper is greatly reduced. Trout love grasshoppers, and I've seen them travel more than a dozen feet to smash one on the surface.

Thinking back, I should've taken a moment to cut my leader back a few feet before tying on the hopper. The typical nine-foot leader I use while trout fishing is tapered—stout on the end that attaches to the fly line, narrowing down to about 5-pound test at the fly—giving it a break strength of about 15 pounds at the halfway point. That is what I should've done, but I didn't. This second bad decision cost me a trout that might've gone twenty-six inches or more.

Drifting my ersatz hopper down the lazy current a few feet downstream of my position, I watched through the crystal-clear water as a leviathan brown trout emerged from underneath an undercut bank less than two rod lengths from where I was standing. Then I watched the fish rise three feet up through the water to intercept the hopper. Because the current was slow, this huge, hook-jawed male had about three full seconds to reach the fly. Keeping in mind the aforementioned bad decisions I made leading up to that moment, in the same amount of time I realized that I am a very stupid man. When I reefed back on the rod and drove the hook home, I knew what the eventual outcome would most likely be, and in my head I was already arranging all the bad words in their proper order so my string of expletives, after the break off, would achieve maximum offensiveness.

The big male brown took my hopper the way really big trout take a fly from the surface. Along with the hopper, he vacuumed enough water into his mouth to cause the water to vortex, and it made the sucking sound a toilet makes at the end of a flush. I'm not kidding. In fly-fishing circles, this is known as a "toilet bowl take." After setting the hook, the big brown simply took his sweet time and slowly swam back under the bank. Heck, he was so big, I doubt he even knew he was hooked. What did I do then? Well, of course I panicked and put too much bend on the rod and snapped the flimsy leader like it was sewing thread.

William Butler Yeats, the great Irish poet and playwright, once wrote, "Being Irish, he had an abiding sense of tragedy, which sustained him through temporary periods of joy." My mom had that quote framed, and it occupied a prominent space on our kitchen wall when I was growing up. Being older now, I understand and appreciate those words more than I ever did as a kid. Hey, if things are going really well, don't worry, because something fairly unpleasant is about to happen.

That sunny late September day marked yet another piscatorial tragedy in my life. Live and learn, right? Well, evidently I'm still working on the learning part. I made another conscious decision to tempt fate with a fly rod, and fate showed up and broke my heart. I thought maybe I'd run down to that stream again before the season closed and throw another Dave's Hopper tied to a heavier leader. Then I thought, *Naw, I bet that fish learned his lesson after making only one bad decision to eat my phony grasshopper.* I have little doubt that that big brown trout is smarter and wiser than I am.

grass

Here is a fact that really is true: I hate mowing. I never had to think too long or hard about why I hate to cut the grass. You see, I grew up with a grandpa and dad who took their lawn care far too seriously. As a matter of fact, Grandpa Kruger won some sort of "Best Lawn in South Minneapolis" award for about ten years running. Grandpa Kruger was one squared-away anal German, let me tell you. When we were growing up, my cousins, brother, and I were not allowed to walk on Grandma and Grandpa Kruger's lawn. Grandpa would keep a close eye on us kids through the windows and yell at us for even looking at his grass. "Um aus dem Gras!" They had a sidewalk that was maybe two feet wide. That's where we were allowed to play, and a game of tag didn't take too long. "You're it . . . you're it . . . you're it . . . Mein Gott, this is stupid! I quit!"

My dad was almost as anal about our yard in Golden Valley. When I was young, Pops would hand me one of those pronged metal dandelion poppers and a five-gallon bucket with instructions to rid the entire lawn of the color yellow. I would sit in one spot and pop about a hundred dandelions, scoot my skinny ass about three feet, then start the whole process again. I know they had weed killer back then, which tells me Dad was more interested in making my weekends miserable than he was in efficiently ridding the lawn of dandelions. By the time I was twelve, I was an expert precision edger of driveways and walkways. How sad is that?

I know hate is a strong word, but my hatred for grass and lawns in general really does go well beyond the more acceptable word, *dislike*. For instance, I dislike curried foods, but I've never once looked at a bowl of peshawari chole and said, "I hate you," or, "You suck," like I do just before pulling the cord on our old Crafts-man mower. See the difference?

There are others like me out there. Christopher Ingraham wrote an article for the *Washington Post* titled "Lawns Are a Soul-Crushing Timesuck and Most of Us Would Be Better Off Without Them." To my way of thinking, the fact that this article was pub-lished in such a highly esteemed fish wrapper as the *Washington Post* lends credibility to my shared hatred for grass. I learned many interesting facts while reading this article, such as that Republi-cans, on average, enjoy cutting their grass more than Democrats. (Wow, that is uncanny, because I'm a card-carrying tax-and-spend knee-jerk liberal.) Or that we spend about seventy hours per year working on our lawns. Did you know that more than 20 percent of the total land area of Massachusetts is covered in grass? Interest-ing facts to some, no doubt, but I don't care, because it would be the same as reading facts about root canal procedures.

A couple of weeks ago, I fired up the mower on a blistering hot day. Prior to that, I checked the local ten-day forecast and was pleased to discover an extended period of bone-dry conditions. I dropped the mower's deck setting from high lush to scalp, then proceeded to cut the grass. This well-timed technique, if properly executed during the months of July and August, will all but as-sure you won't have to mow your lawn again for the better part of a month. In a couple of days, your water-starved, brown crunchy grass will fall into an induced coma–like state until a good rain comes. Hey, you're welcome for that tip.

Nowadays my son Anders typically mows the lawn. I use the word *lawn* pretty loosely. It is bordered by pine trees on three sides with lots of pine needles that fall to the ground and render the soil too acidic to grow much grass. From a ratio standpoint, I have to believe our lawn is probably half grass and half weeds, so I've held off using what is known as "weed and feed," for fear that following an application, we'd be left with something resembling a dusty, weed-choked elementary school playground.

When Anders mows the lawn, I leave him be. The evil cycle of anal-retentiveness must be broken, right? Are there spots and strips of grass he misses? Yep. Do I give a rat's ass? Nope. Have I witnessed Anders running behind the mower in an attempt to finish cutting the grass as fast as humanly possible so he can move on to more stimulating and desired activities? Yes I have, and again, I don't care. Just make sure the blade speed setting is on the rabbit and not the turtle while you're running, Son.

straightaway grouse

They do their best to make us look downright foolish at times, unnerving us as they explode from the ground or a perch overhead, their startling whir of wings designed to disorient any would-be predators.

What's more, they have an uncanny ability to fly where we least expect them to fly, and too often they seem to anticipate where a particular flight path will almost always guarantee their safe escape. Of course, I'm describing the ruffed grouse, a bird that very rarely loses "situational awareness" while airborne.

If you do decide to walk the woods for grouse, keep in mind that these birds can quickly achieve speeds nearing thirty miles per hour, all while artfully dodging tree trunks and branches. Anybody who hunts this bird can attempt to explain how tough they are to hit with a shotgun, but you really need to experience the moment firsthand, when bird and hunter converge at that critical moment when skill, luck, and fate intersect for a brief second or two. If the hunter can somehow mindfully slow down in that moment and swing the gun true, then the scale begins to tip in the hunter's favor.

My family and I spent a long MEA weekend up at our cottage, located just south of Manitowish Waters in north-central Wisconsin. During the month of October and early November, the grouse is the undisputed king of the forest, drawing hunters to the Northwoods in search of this highly prized and respected game bird.

For a grouse hunter like me, there is no gift more welcome than a bird that flies straightaway after being flushed. Hunting in and around Vilas County in northern Wisconsin near our family cottage is always a fall favorite for Anders, Augie, and me.

Personally, I enjoy the process of studying plat maps and other resources that delineate public and private lands. From there, it's a matter of driving along county and somewhat obscure back roads in search of walking trails that might put me near preferred grouse habitat. After a few years, I've come to rely on some pretty dependable coverts that hold feeding birds season after season—places where I'm always kept on high alert when walking them during the early evening hours.

Finding a good grouse gun, using proper chokes, and choosing (or handloading) effective loads is only part of the recipe for success. The ability to almost instantaneously shoulder a gun and point and swing it properly—all within the tight confines of grouse cover—is where the rubber really meets the road.

They say that if you can hit one bird for every six you flush, you're shooting pretty well. I downed two birds that weekend, but I'm hesitant to tell you how many empty hulls I extracted from the breech of my side-by-side and placed in the front left pocket of my vest. Let's just say there were a few more than a dozen. I won't go so far as to define "a few."

One thing I was reminded of that weekend is that you simply cannot walk too slowly for grouse. The birds I shot flushed while I was standing motionless, anticipating their move. One of the most effective methods to flush birds is to walk for five to ten seconds, then suddenly stop. Grouse, if they can't see you, get quite nervous when a possible predator or hunter stops making noise near their cover.

I've said it before and it's worth repeating: there is no such thing as a bad grouse hunt. If for no other reason, it's the perfect excuse to walk the woods and trails during the prettiest time of the year. And there is always the anticipation of a flushing grouse that, no matter how many years we've been hunting them, makes our hearts skip a beat and our pulses race.

On Saturday evening of that weekend, before leaving for home the following day, we bowed our heads and gave thanks at the dinner table. On that day, I was particularly thankful for a pair of grouse that flew straightaway.

THE TRUTH CAN BE A VERY SUBJECTIVE THING

As I get older, I find it easier, and oftentimes quite convenient, to dabble in the nebulous and ill-defined areas of the truth, where hunting and fishing are concerned.

You probably think that's just a fancy way of saying I'm a liar. I'm not a liar. Well, not in the strictest sense of the word. It's not like I regularly drag the truth into a dark alley by the scruff of the neck and rough it up every chance I get. To my way of thinking, lying involves patently false statements and an intention to deceive. Hey, after I'm through talking, it's certainly not my fault if folks hear part of a story and form their own false impressions.

The other day I told a friend about a trip my brother and I made last Saturday to the Mille Lacs Wildlife Management Area in search of grouse. I recall saying something like, "Well, I had my portable GPS clipped to my vest and discovered that Jim and I walked nearly six miles. Six miles! Man, my legs are still sore today. Oh, by the way, we did manage to put three birds up, which was good." You see how that works? It's not open-ended, and it doesn't prompt the other guy to pry too much regarding details. The fact that my brother and I didn't put a single one of the three aforementioned birds up and in the proverbial game bag is neither here nor there.

Another slippery tactic is to take a vague statement of half fact like the one I just mentioned and immediately follow it up with a diversionary question of your own: "So, you been seeing birds where you're at? Yeah, I've heard mixed reports myself. I heard the Arrowhead and north-central brood survey numbers are down. Must've been a tough spring on the chicks, eh?" Honest to God, confound other hunters with juicy lines like that and they'll dummy up faster than Mortimer Snerd. No one will question your savant-like knowledge. Hell, take it a bit further and mention things like frequent spring rain events during the brood-rearing season and chicks having a tough time thermoregulating. Thermo-whaa? Yes sir, sprinkle some legitimate biological hocus-pocus in there for good measure, and you could net yourself a cold beer or two from admiring fans in any tavern.

Like I mentioned, sometimes it just makes good sense to withhold details from fellow anglers and hunters, if for no other reason than to keep your secret fishing and hunting spots secret awhile longer. The trick is to govern your mouth and stop yourself a hair shy of whipping out a map and stabbing your finger on those places where you've recently enjoyed success.

Remember that facts and details are highly malleable and oftentimes subjective at best. Tell a guy you shot a buck and move on . . . the quicker the better. The fact that your particular buck's antlers were mere nubbins and hadn't yet sprouted is trivial. Or go ahead and tell folks you recently caught some dandy walleyes, but be prepared to suddenly feign a groin pull and excuse yourself from the conversation. You're done. That's enough information. You know a "dandy" walleye—from an eating standpoint—measures about fourteen to eighteen inches. The fact that whoever's listening thinks a "dandy" walleye measures around twenty-six inches is no concern of yours. You see what I mean. Facts are, at best, highly subjective, aren't they?

Maybe I missed my calling as a politician. After years of practice, I've developed a pretty good poker face. I'm sure I could look into a camera lens and solemnly promise lower taxes and affordable health care to my fellow Americans as well as the next candidate. The difference between what comes out of my mouth and the mouths of guys like Trump and Biden is that nobody can run to FactCheck.org to authenticate my hunting and fishing stories. On second thought, maybe I'll rethink a burgeoning political career.

september on the stream

During the month of September, just as our Minnesota woods begin to burst with color at the onset of fall, so do the trout that inhabit our streams and rivers, as they prepare for the spawning season. Male brown and brook trout transform themselves into what can only be described as an artist's embellishment, using the most intense red, yellow, and purple hues from the palette: scarlet bellies, with olive flanks speckled with halos of golden spots as bright and radiant as the fallen maple, aspen, and oak leaves that are swept downstream.

After the warm summer months, when insect hatches are infrequent and the fish lethargic, September marks a special time of year for the trout angler. It is a brief month of memorable fishing before the close of the regular season, when trout are compelled to feed aggressively in preparation for their physically strenuous late-season spawn. As an added bonus to the angler, this period of transition and productive fishing often occurs when the weather is nothing short of idyllic. Throwing large terrestrial patterns such as grasshoppers and beetles on a long, light tippet over gin-clear water is, in and of itself, a supreme challenge, and it's common at this time of year to see fish travel a number of feet to savagely take an easy meal that has seemingly fallen from the bank. Oftentimes, I think of Dick Blalock's clever quote just before making a long upstream cast to a fish holding in the current: "These brook trout will strike any fly you present, provided you don't get close enough to present it."

A colorful and chunky brook trout fooled by a big bushy dry fly on the upper reaches of the Stewart River, a tributary of Lake Superior along Minnesota's North Shore.

Every year, I look forward to the fall stream trout season in anticipation of that unforgettable moment when I gaze upon the first brightly colored fish caught in September. These fish undergo a spectacular visual transformation that marks the change of seasons and the cyclical rhythm of nature. At this time of year, I truly believe that every fish I hook and bring to the net is a reward, a bonus.

If you've been fortunate enough to briefly hold and admire one of these living works of art under the September sun, you'll understand that I feel most fortunate and thankful to be a trout angler. I appreciate the beauty that can be found in nature, and to put it quite simply, there isn't another species of fish that rivals the sheer splendor of a colorful trout dressed in its fall finery.

A BIG BUCK

W e settled into our portable stands about a half hour before sunrise. Less than fifteen minutes later I heard the loud report of Anders's 12-gauge Remington slug gun shatter the quiet and stillness of the predawn. The sound was shocking and it startled me. Being curious but mostly concerned, I climbed down from my stand and yelled to Anders that I was headed his way. When I approached the base of Anders's tree, I looked up and asked him if he'd shot a deer. "Yeah," he replied. "After I got settled in I glanced over my left shoulder and saw a buck with big antlers crawling under the pines. He was crawling with his belly right next to the ground. With all the grass and pine needles, I never heard him. It was lucky I decided to look that way."

It was too soon after he had taken the shot to begin tracking the animal. It is typically the case that a wounded deer will continue to move away from anything it feels is pursuing it, so we waited. It gave us time to talk about how the shot was taken and whether Anders felt he put a good hit on the deer. Anders remarked, "I saw him early enough to pick a spot in a clearing between two pines, and I think I got him right in the vitals after his shoulder moved past the sight. Plus, he was only about thirty feet away, so there's no way I could've missed him."

After the sun came up, it took us an uncomfortable amount of time to discover any sign that Anders had in fact hit the deer. Finally, after we'd systematically fanned out yet another ten yards, I reluctantly expressed the possibility that perhaps Anders had

This big buck was crawling under pine boughs to keep from walking through an open section of meadow on a friend's property near Scandia, Minnesota. Witnessing a big buck crawl under objects or through short grass is somewhat rare. Anders was fortunate to have seen this firsthand. It is unusual behavior like this that helps big bucks survive through numerous hunting seasons.

missed the buck. It was shortly after that that I found a few spots of blood about thirty yards from the point of impact; when this happens, it usually indicates there was no exit wound on the deer. The farther we followed it, the blood trail became more and more evident. When Anders and I finally saw the deer he had shot, after tracking it about one hundred yards through a dense stand of pines, the sheer size of the buck and its antlers were truly a sight to behold. From twenty yards out, when we got our first good look at it, we knew Anders had taken a very nice buck indeed.

As we neared the animal, my focus was riveted on the sizable antlers. They seemed to grow with every step we took toward the buck. Were they typical antlers? Was any part of the rack damaged or broken? These questions are common and often race through the mind of a deer hunter approaching a downed buck. About the only thing I could think to say when we finally reached the deer was, "Oh my gosh. Look at the size of this thing! This is the biggest deer any of us have ever taken in all the years we've been hunting out here." The last part of that statement was true by a long shot.

We estimated the deer's weight to be around 230 to 240 pounds—a massive nine-pointer with an inside spread of twenty-four inches. When Anders's grandpa Ron showed up with his pickup truck about a half hour later and got his first look at the buck, he said, "Jiminy Christmas! That is the biggest deer I've ever seen!" It was a struggle for the three of us to muscle the buck up and into the bed of Ron's truck.

Just about every deer season I seem to do pretty well, with the last few being remarkably good. I was lucky enough to take a few eight-pointers and a nice ten-pointer. The ten-point rack hangs in our dining room, and I was convinced at the time I took that deer he would be a tough one to beat. Boy, was I wrong. It turns out my ten-point rack fits quite easily inside Anders's nine-pointer.

As it turned out, I didn't even see a deer this past season, and that was fine with me. What made my own season perfectly satisfying was the fact that I was a part of Anders's experience in harvesting his huge buck. The excitement and anticipation he and I felt as we worked together to track the animal, then approach it in wide-eyed wonderment, was just as fulfilling to me as if I had taken the deer myself.

I usually prepare and plaque our antlers myself, but decided against it in the case of Anders's rack. I didn't want to screw it up somehow, so I took it to a reputable taxidermist in Forest Lake to do the work. When I told the taxidermist the story behind the deer, he got caught up in the excitement, too, and promised he'd do everything he could do to get the project done by Christmas.

True to his word, he called me in the evening on December 23 to let me know he'd just finished the job. Needless to say, the sight of those newly mounted antlers hanging on the living room wall on Christmas morning was a nice gift indeed.

It seemed fitting that one of the younger hunters in our group now holds the big buck crown. But as happy as I am for Anders, I can't help but think of the age-old saying: records are meant to be broken. Our family is quite competitive, so I'm being honest when I say that Augie and I have every intention of shooting a bigger buck than Anders's nine-pointer next season.

A Visit With an Old Friend

The two-track road leading to the stream hadn't changed much since the last time I had traveled it. I realized that nearly eighteen years had passed, and my vivid memory of the road's path and surrounding terrain hadn't faded. The road was cut through the rolling evergreen forest in the early 1980s to make way for the large logging trucks and machinery necessary to harvest the trees and move them to nearby sawmills. Most of the old-growth pines had long since disappeared, and in their place stood a second-growth coniferous forest planted in tidy rows, intermingling with aspens and poplars. For thousands of years, the skyward view along this path had been the soaring green cathedral of a dense pine canopy, but that was quickly lost to logging over the past couple of decades. I listened to the distant crescendo of buzzing cicadas and the whirring of grasshoppers taking flight; the noonday sun felt hot on my neck and face as I walked.

The trek was long but the road remained sufficiently open and the going was fairly easy. In the past the only thing I felt while walking to this stream was the anticipation of getting there, but now I felt the passage of the years in my legs and back, making me wonder what I'd do if I suffered a bad fall or some such mishap out in the middle of nowhere. I also wondered if the trout would be where I expected them to be, occupying the holes in the bends of the stream and the deeper riffles and undercuts.

There was a pretty good chance the stream might not be there any longer, and a better chance that the stream wouldn't

After a long hike the brook trout were still there, years after I had last fished this unnamed creek in northern Minnesota's Superior National Forest.

be anything like I remembered it. Or, if the stream was still there, perhaps there wouldn't be any fish in it to catch.

The mile of open land halted abruptly at the edge of a dense pine forest, which I could see from a distance as I crested high points along the road. Twenty years earlier, men and machinery stopped their northward progress where a straight line of old-growth white pines still stands defiantly. My backpack, containing waders, boots, lunch, and fly-fishing gear, was becoming heavy on my shoulders, so I decided to rest once I reached the tall pines.

The moment I entered the forest, I noticed a marked drop in temperature and the abundance of bird noises. The birds seemed to be everywhere in and among the pine bows and, like me, sought refuge from the bright sun and heat. Birdsongs sounded different among the tall pines; their chirps and warbles didn't stay in the air very long before the trees absorbed them as effectively as acoustic tiles.

Following a short rest, I began walking again and after ten minutes knew that the stream wasn't far. The forest floor began to drop quite sharply, and I could hear and see the moving water below. I took a diagonal route down the bank to the stream, using the small trees and saplings for handholds. When I got to the water's edge I was pleased to see that the little stream remained, just as I hoped it would. Slowly walking along the soft bank, I stared into the deeper runs and riffles and could see brook trout moving sideways, finning in the current, their mottled olive backs dark against the light sandy streambed. One fish caught sight of me and quickly shot upstream, abandoning its feeding lie to seek refuge under a root wad.

Sometimes I wonder what forces are at work that compel us and lead us back to particular places. Perhaps it's necessary for each of us to revisit memorable places from our past from time to time, if only to hope that they continue to exist. And, if we can free our minds of thoughts in the here and now, we just might be lucky enough to experience the enchanted emotions of our youth once more.

A couple of summers ago, I returned to just such a place. For reasons I can't fully explain, I felt compelled to walk the same road and hear the same sounds and take in the same smells and catch wild brook trout in an old familiar stream that few people knew about or cared enough to fish.

Going back to that small stream felt comfortable, and after stringing up my little six-foot brush rod and plucking a colorful Royal Wulff dry fly out of my fly box, it felt like only a day or two had passed since I'd last fished there. The anticipation of catching that first colorful brook trout felt the same as it did eighteen years earlier.

It's reassuring to find yourself spending time with an old friend you haven't seen in years and discover that your relationship hasn't changed too much. Of course, this experience can't be fully appreciated and cherished unless we ourselves don't fundamentally change too much either.

unlocking a secret

My in-laws own a cottage on a northern Wisconsin lake near Manitowish Waters. The lake is gin clear, as they say; deep; and loaded with big smallmouth bass—or so the local bait shop owner kept telling me. I had fished the lake with marginal success for a decade, regularly catching smaller fish. All that changed a few years ago when I made a startling discovery on a bright, sunny day without a lick of wind.

I was in a jon boat, slowly rowing away from the shoreline and peering over the gunwale while viewing sunfish in the shallower water. At twenty-two feet of depth—just at the point where the lake's bottom was becoming tough to see—I saw them. Or I thought I saw them.

I remember resting my chin on an oar and staring straight down into the water, being careful not to cause any movement that could ripple the surface and distort my vision. Doing this, I was able to see them: large shadowed forms moving slowly along the bottom, some of them looking remarkably like overinflated footballs with fins. I thought, *Yikes, those can't be . . . yes they are. They're huge smallies!*

Everyone else who I'd seen fish this lake fished for bass the same way—including me—until I made my discovery. We'd throw spinnerbaits or deep-diving crankbaits toward shore during the morning or evening hours, stealthily using the low light in hopes of catching larger fish that might be cruising the shallows.

In the past, I've done pretty well live-bait rigging for walleye, so naturally I began to toy with the idea of deep-drifting leeches and fathead minnows along the bottom behind a slip sinker, putting the bait smack-dab in the faces of these big bass. Looking at these fish surely wasn't going to put any in the boat, so I got to shore, grabbed a couple of Styrofoam buckets, and pushed the speed limit all the way to the bait shop. I'd ordered a half pound of leeches and two dozen minnows when the shop owner asked, "Gonna give the walleyes a shot?" Being an experienced angler and fairly adept in the art of bald-faced lying, I replied with a poker face, "Yep."

Well, I'm not usually the guy who thinks too far outside the box when it comes to fishing, but I guess I sort of unlocked one of the lake's secrets on that particular day. It turned out that applying a tried-and-true walleye tactic for these deep-water bass was nothing short of incredible. While others continued to ply the shallows before and after the sun was high in the sky, I began to wait until late morning to drag large minnows and leeches along the bottom in the sunshine, usually in water twenty-four to thirty-two-feet deep.

To this day, this tactic never, ever fails to entice and fool these bruisers. I've had unseen behemoths snap 8-pound test line like it was sewing thread. Last summer, my son Anders had a smallmouth hooked and nearly to the boat that, after I briefly caught a glimpse of the fish, made my knees shake. And earlier this season, my wife's uncle saw a smallie he figured was all of twenty-four inches jump skyward and cleanly break his 10-pound mono at the barrel swivel.

My tactic continues to produce plenty of nice fish, and I'm happy to report that the bass aren't onto us yet. We once fished during a severe cold front with a sharp north wind that didn't push the mercury much above fifty degrees for three straight days. Even when the fishing wasn't supposed to be worth a tinker, we mercilessly pounded the bejesus out of the big smallies. They're still powerless over the seductive ways of the live-bait rig.

BUeTeR'S SaLMon camP

E very summer an old casting-instructor friend of mine, John Bueter, has invited me to his annual Bueter's Salmon Camp, traditionally held in late September or early October in his home-town of Baldwin, Michigan. The river is the famed Pere Marquette, and king salmon are the target.

Beginning in late August through early October, literally tens of thousands of king salmon make their spawning run up the Pere Marquette from Lake Michigan, eventually inhabiting the entire sixty-four-mile length of the river.

As Salmon Camp drew nearer, John sent subsequent emails to friends with news that there were reports of high numbers of thirty-to-forty-pound fish in the river. I've hooked and battled plenty of six-to-twelve-pound steelhead in North Shore tributaries here in Minnesota and on the Brule River in Wisconsin, and I know how those fish can test every bit of your equipment and skill as a fly angler. Rods, reels, lines, and knots can be strained to their limits against such quarry, so I was having a hard time imagining what would be necessary to subdue the size of fish John described in his emails.

This past fall I decided that I simply had to make that trip to Baldwin to John's Salmon Camp, but not before inundating John with numerous questions over the phone: What sort of sink-tip lines are you running? What pound test leaders should I bring along? Are there some fly patterns I absolutely have to have in my box? John's response was fairly succinct and straight to the point, which is what I've always appreciated about him. "Seven to ten inches per second loop-to-loop or integrated sink-tips, straight fluorocarbon leaders, Coal Cars, Green Butt Skunks, and Crystal Bullet Flies. Size four hooks max and the gap can't be wider than half an inch. Just get your ass here and we'll take care of you. Oh, and leave your seven-weight rods at home unless you want them snapped in two. Bring your big guns. We'll be catching some very big fish."

Well, a response like that is all a fella like me needs to hear.

So off we went—me and my son Augie, along with my pal Scott Frischmon and his son Mike. Driving straight through the night, we arrived at Bueter's Salmon Camp Friday morning. We were all tired but ready and eager to fish.

One fellow at camp could sense we really wanted to hit the water, so he enthusiastically volunteered to take us to an area of the river known as Gleasons Landing. We arrived at a trailhead and began to walk through a stand of pines to a section of water where the trail itself was quite high along a steep bank. Below us we saw a number of enormous male kings, bellies to the bottom, finning in the current. Above that group of fish, we saw a shallow gravel bar inhabited by a lone female.

We had to wait awhile for some other anglers to leave that stretch of water before we could give it a shot. This was a bit unlike anything I'd experienced before. I've swung a lot of flies in my time, but never to giant salmon that I could plainly see twenty to thirty feet away from me. No doubt they could plainly see us, too, but the name of the game when fishing salmon in a river is waiting for an instinctual—or "reflex"—bite. Salmon don't have eating on their mind after they enter a river to spawn, and the eventual outcome for these fish is that they literally spawn and die. This is often a two-to-three-month process, so for Lake Michigan tributaries such as the Pere Marquette and Manistee, the king salmon run occurs in waves, beginning in late August and ending sometime in October.

We hadn't been fishing that spot for too long before I tied into a big male. I had swung my #4 Crystal Bullet in front of this particular fish perhaps ten times before he decided to kick to his right and inhale the fly. When I saw the king close his mouth, I pointed the rod tip almost directly at the fish and strip-set the hook firmly once, twice, and a third time for good measure. It took a few seconds before the giant king felt the pressure and realized he was hooked; then all hell broke loose. The big king shot straight upstream about one hundred feet, my reel's drag whining and hissing in protest. Then the king jumped a number of feet out of the water, turned tail, and began a blistering run downstream, with me working the reel handle as fast as I could in an attempt to get line back on the spool. I have never seen a hooked thirty-plus-pound fish leave the water like that, and it sounded like somebody chucked a cinder block into the water when it landed. This fish launched itself into the air two more times before Scott was able to net it a fair distance downstream. When he initially saw the fish he said, "I'm not sure it'll fit in the net." But it did, and that fish marked the beginning of two days of incredible king salmon fishing on the Pere Marquette River.

Augie picked up a dandy shortly after I'd caught a couple, and the following day, both Mike and Augie caught some absolute bruisers of their own. Some of the fish were so large, the boys could barely hold them up horizontally for the photos.

On our drive home we all agreed it was the best fishing trip we'd ever taken, and that wasn't just based on the fishing. Our experiences at John's Salmon Camp were as incredible as the fishing itself. Meeting new friends, sharing tales of the day's catches around the campfire, and the mentorship and unreserved sharing of information was invaluable. The guys we met put us on fish and let us know precisely how best to catch them.

We'll make the journey to Bueter's Salmon Camp again this fall, and for as many years as we can after that. John's motto for the

Swinging flies to enormous king salmon on the Pere Marquette River in Michigan recalibrated our idea of what a big fish looked like. If not fought properly and with a fair measure of respect, these kings are perfectly capable of snapping heavier fly rods in two.

past twenty-nine years of his camp's existence has been, "This is too much fun to keep to ourselves." Scott and I have a few others in mind who would love to experience the world-class king salmon fishing the Pere Marquette has to offer.

STEELHEADING
THE NORTH SHORE

A few weeks ago I fished for steelhead with my sons, Anders and Augie. Anders is finishing his undergraduate work at the University of Minnesota–Duluth, while Augie is approaching the end of his junior year of high school. Anders is an avid steelhead angler, and due to his proximity to numerous tributaries along the North Shore of Lake Superior, he is able to fish for steelhead often in the spring, when the fish leave the Big Lake and make their spawning run into the rivers.

On that day, Anders told us he would not rig a rod and reel for himself, but rather spend his time on the water as our guide of sorts, pointing out productive stretches and specific spots that held fish where he had recently fished.

Our first stop was the Stewart River, located a short distance up the shore from the city of Two Harbors. The spawn was essentially over, but the Stewart and other tributaries still held a fair number of "fallback" fish that would readily take well-drifted bug and egg patterns. These post-spawn fish actively feed during the time between spawning and their return downstream to the expanse of Lake Superior.

With the water low and clear, the steelhead were occupying deeper runs and water shaded by the steep volcanic rock walls common to these rivers. Anders pointed out just such a run to Augie, and Augie in turn made a perfect quartering cast up into the

Anders (left) with a big thumbs-up after Augie hooked and landed this large steelhead on the Stewart River along the North Shore of Lake Superior near Two Harbors, Minnesota. Anders put us on some nice fish that day.

head of the run. The egg pattern quickly sank, bumping and tumbling its way along the riverbed, with the strike indicator floating on the surface, marking its journey with the current. Suddenly, the indicator shot upstream, and Augie instinctively stripped line and set the hook. His 8-weight rod throbbed under the strain of a heavy fish. It took full advantage of the swift water, peeling line off the reel as it made two strong runs downstream. Applying side pressure after dropping the tip of the rod down next to the water, Augie was finally able to steer the brute toward the near shore. After getting some line back on the reel and working the fish to the surface, Anders was then able to wade out and slip his net under a thirty-inch male "buck" steelhead. This was Augie's first wild steelhead, and it was a big one. Anders joked that Augie might fish a long time before he lands another one that size.

It was a very memorable outing. Anders, despite his initial plan to act as our guide only, simply could not help himself and did occasionally take some casts, landing an additional fish on the Stewart before we tried our luck farther north on the Split Rock River. There, Anders and I brought two additional fish to hand.

It is interesting to think about how we learn to do things well, particularly over a long period of time, incremental improvements that are built upon over the course of many years. In the case of Anders and Augie, I don't recall a lot of instances in which I formally taught them things like how to cast or tie a knot, choose a proper fly, or read water to determine where fish are most likely to be, but I assume I've done enough of it over the years. Beyond those teaching moments, their progression in this sport no doubt happened gradually over time, through long hours and days of trial and error on the water, and maybe more important, trial and success on the water. Knowing which fly patterns work well and quickly identifying productive water in a river are skills that must be learned over the course of seasons. There are no shortcuts.

It was fortunate that Anders decided to rig up only two rods on that day. I gave Anders the second rod from time to time and encouraged him to fish alongside his brother, which in turn allowed me to stand back and simply observe them. I imagined where I would place my cast in the most productive water, and invariably either Anders or Augie would cast to those very spots.

I experienced a moment of clarity on that day. A moment when it dawned on me that I had raised two fine fly anglers. I appreciated what my Montana friend Phil Maxwell wrote to me after he learned of our successful outing and saw a number of photos. He said my wife and I had raised two fine boys who fish. I like the sound of that even better.

In Norman Maclean's novel *A River Runs Through It*, Reverend Maclean describes Norman's younger brother, Paul, as beautiful while he fished. I read this book perhaps three or four years after it was published in 1979, and it took me many years after that to realize what Reverend Maclean's use of the word "beautiful" meant. He did not use it to describe exclusively an aesthetic, but rather that Paul had achieved a considerable measure of grace in the sport of fly-fishing, that he had seamlessly infused himself into the rhythm of nature on a trout river.

I experienced a similar enlightening revelation on that day fishing with Anders and Augie. An epiphany of sorts. While I sat on the rocky bank of the Split Rock River, I was able to witness two fine anglers who indeed brought a considerable measure of beauty and grace to the sport of fly-fishing.

TO THE BRULE AND SIOUX AND BACK

There are times when I am compelled to travel unreasonable distances in the span of a single day to experience outstanding fishing. I'm experiencing one of those moments of weakness right now. Following an excruciatingly long winter, I'm finalizing plans on this glorious seventy-degree day to travel to the snow-covered woods of northern Wisconsin to do battle with wild steelhead that have begun to nose into Superior's tributaries to spawn.

I'm thankful to have a friend in mind for this trip. We'll drive together through the predawn hours this Sunday morning in order to maximize the hours spent on the rivers we hope are not too high or fast to fish. On Superior's tributaries, snowmelt triggers the Big Lake's migrating fish to enter river mouths in search of gravel beds on which to lay their eggs. In the case of spawning steelhead, timing truly is everything, and there are far more combinations of conditions and factors that can negatively affect the run.

Our plan is to first scout and fish the Bois Brule north of Highway 2. We'll gladly stay put if the conditions are favorable and the steelhead are occupying their usual haunts. If not, we'll look at the Onion and Sioux Rivers that flow into Chequamegon Bay south of the Apostle Islands.

I hope that my ten-foot, 7-weight rod has the backbone to turn a hard-charging thirty-inch "chromer" after it decides to quickly burn a hundred feet of fly line off my reel.

I hope that I'll be fortunate enough to see wild steelhead on gravel beds in the throes of their annual spawning ritual. And I hope I'm quiet enough and my first cast is accurate enough to fool a smaller male "buck" relegated to a downstream position with a brightly colored yarn fly.

Spring marks the season of hope. With the snowmelt rivers rise, some of them northward; their flows quicken as they rush to meet Superior.

With every drift of a carefully chosen fly through promising waters, anglers on northern rivers will hope for a sign that they've fooled their quarry, and in doing so, hope can—and often does—spring eternal. Some days, when the fishing is particularly good, it is only the waning light and thoughts of others waiting at home for our safe return that interrupts our reverie.

Every year and for many years to come, I hope to be on a river when the snows melt and the rivers rise.

Acknowledgments

I would like to offer my heartfelt gratitude to my managing editor Laurie Buss Herrmann, and the rest of the team at Beaver's Pond Press, as well as to Ryan Scheife for his creative work at Mayfly Design.

I hope that you enjoyed reading *Da Fishi Code*. It was my hope that some of the pieces allowed you to vicariously accompany me on some of my most memorable days on the water and in the woods with family and friends. As far as the sillier stories and my overactive imagination are concerned, I thank you for your indulgence. Above all else, I hope many of these short stories put a smile on your face.

If you enjoyed reading *Da Fishi Code*, please help spread the word to your own friends and family through Facebook and other social media platforms. For any debut author, there is no greater honor than word-of-mouth recommendations from readers.